THE REVELATION OF JESUS CHRIST

THE REVELATION OF JESUS CHRIST

A lamp to our feet and a light to our path

Tony Green

ARTHUR H. STOCKWELL LTD
Torrs Park   Ilfracombe   Devon
Established 1898
www.ahstockwell.co.uk

British Library Cataloguing-in-Publication Data.
A catalogue record for this book is available
from the British Library.

Arthur H. Stockwell Ltd bears no responsibility
for the accuracy of information recorded in this book.

Scripture taken from The Message.
Copyright © 1993, 1994, 1995, 1996, 2000, 2001, 2002.
Used by permission of NavPress Publishing Group.

ISBN 978-0-7223-3978-7
Printed in Great Britain by
Arthur H. Stockwell Ltd
Torrs Park   Ilfracombe
Devon

CONTENTS

INTRODUCTION

Thank you for allowing me to share with you the thoughts that have come to me from this wonderful book, The Revelation of Jesus Christ, the last book in the Bible.

In putting these thoughts together, I have kept the following in mind:

1. I am not a teacher so it will not be a teaching book or a textbook.
2. I am using the Message translation of the Bible in order to keep a flow in the text. Those looking for chapter and verse quotations I am afraid will be disappointed.
3. As all the scripture quotations are from the Message translation, I intend to use the way in which the writer to the Hebrews quotes the scripture, stating it is written or giving the name or writer of the book not the chapter and verse.
4. When quoting, I will sometimes say I heard or read someone saying or writing the following. This is because often I simply do not remember who wrote or said what I am quoting.
5. This is a very subjective work; I am recording what I have experienced of the Lord over many years.
6. I shall keep the chapters short so they can be easily read and thought over.

Chapter 1

JESUS IS ALIVE
Revelation 1

The Lord Jesus states to John when comforting him, "I'm Alive. I died, but I came to life, and my life is now forever."

This book is a declaration that Jesus is alive and speaking to his churches. Nebuchadnezzar saw a great image, but it was lifeless, speechless. The one John saw was very much alive and his voice commanded the attention of the churches, the occupants of heaven and the nations of the world.

As we experience the Lord Jesus in our lives, like John we worship him as the one who is, 'Loyal Witness, Firstborn from the dead, Ruler of all earthly kings. Glory and strength to Christ, who loves us, who blood-washed our sins from our lives, who made us a Kingdom, Priests for his Father, forever', and declare, "Yes, he's on his way!" And with the great company in heaven we declare, "Worthy! Take the scroll, open its seals. Slain! Paying in blood, you bought men and women, Bought them back from all over the earth, Bought them back for God. Then you made them a Kingdom, Priests for our God, Priest-kings to rule over the earth". "The slain Lamb is worthy! Take the power, the wealth, the wisdom, the strength! Take the honour, the glory, the blessing!" "To the One on the Throne! To the Lamb! The blessing, the honour, the glory, the strength, For age after age after age."

Jesus and the disciples were together for the last time after he had proved he was alive for forty days. As Luke tells us in the Book of Acts, 'After his death, he presented himself alive to them in many different settings over a period of forty days. In face-to-face meetings, he talked to them about things concerning the kingdom of God.' They asked him, "Master, are you going to restore the kingdom to Israel now? Is this the time?" He told them, "You don't get to know the time. Timing is the Father's business." Not long after this Jesus was taken from the disciples in a cloud that took him out of their sight. Before he left them he told them again that the Holy Spirit would come to them and they would be witnesses in Jerusalem, Judaea and then to the ends of the world. But Mark tells us Jesus was also working with them: 'And the disciples went everywhere preaching, the Master working right with them, validating the Message with indisputable evidence.' In the Book of Acts Luke goes on to tell us how this happened and ends with Paul in Rome saying that the gospel is now going out to the Gentile nations and they will receive it. The historical account in the Book of Acts teaches us that those who believed in Jesus as their personal saviour would meet together often every day of the week, but weekly on Sunday in order to worship the Lord and that these meetings were called churches. The letters of the New Testament are the teaching that the apostles gave to these churches, teaching on the gospel message and on living for the Lord as his saved people in the communities in which they lived. A major part of the message of the gospel is that Jesus is coming again. We are brought to the close of the written word of God with a revelation given to the churches of what must take place right up to and then after the coming again of Jesus the Messiah.

The churches just sixty or so years after the death, resurrection and ascension of the Lord Jesus were suffering persecution and in a mess. There was only one apostle of the original twelve still alive – John – and he was an elderly man. He lived on an island, suffering persecution for his faith in

Jesus. This last eye witness, who was chosen to be a witness of all that he saw from the beginning of Jesus's ministry after his baptism by John the Baptist right up to his ascension, would not be on this earth for much longer. The Lord Jesus had a final word for his churches to complete the written word of God for his people, and John was to write down all he saw in a revelation given in the form of symbolic visions. It was to comfort the people of God as they lived for him in this increasingly wicked world. John saw in this revelation a message that he would record for the churches of the Lord Jesus Christ.

It seems to me that the Book of Revelation is the response of the God of all comfort to the needs of his churches as they were struggling with doctrinal issues, immorality, bad government of the churches and persecution from the Roman state and the Jewish authorities. Therefore we should read the revelation as a pastoral letter from the Lord Jesus. God gave the revelation to answer the questions that were in the minds of those early Christians. John himself records for us at the beginning and end of the book, 'I, Jesus, sent my Angel to testify to these things for the churches. I'm the Root and Branch of David, the Bright Morning Star.' The book closes with John's reminder that the 'grace of the Master Jesus is with all of you'.

The book will be for all time a guide to the churches so that the Lord's people will be able to say, "It is Jesus himself through whom I can see where I'm going; he throws a beam of light on my way forward."

I propose to look for the message that Jesus has for us in each of the visions given to John that make up this revelation. These messages to the churches told them how they should respond to the Lord and to one another, then how they should respond to the way the world treated them, and the revelation foretold the amazing future awaiting them with the Lord in the redeemed heaven and earth, where there would never again be an invasion by Satan and sin.

The first verse of the book states, 'A revealing of Jesus, the Messiah.' John had last seen Jesus some sixty or so years before, as he was ascending back to heaven. He had seen Jesus then as he had known him for three years before his death on the Cross and then for forty days after his resurrection. Now Jesus as he had been, hidden from sight, was being revealed to John in a symbolic vision of who he is and his function as King Priest to the churches and King of Kings to the nations of the world. The word translated as *revelation* here, we are told by those who study languages, is 'used of events by which things or states or persons hitherto withdrawn from view are made visible to all'.

This last remaining eye witness of Jesus while he was here on earth could say, "I know in this symbolic vision it was Jesus the Messiah I was looking at – the one who constantly spoke of himself as the Messiah by the title 'Son of Man'." He tells us in Chapter 1 of the Book of Revelation that, after praying one Sunday, he became aware that he was taken over by the Holy Spirit in an unusual manner. He heard a voice telling him he was to write what he saw in a book and send it to seven churches. 'I turned around to see who was speaking to me,' he tells us, and 'I saw a gold menorah with seven branches, and in the centre, the Son of Man, in a robe and gold breastplate.'

Seeing Jesus in this symbolic form, expressing his deity, authority and incisive wisdom, John sees him first in relationship to his churches.

May the mighty creative power of the risen Lord penetrate our minds and hearts to be among those who, it is said, defeated Satan through the blood of the Lamb and the bold word of their witness. They weren't in love with themselves; they were willing to die for Christ.

Allow me to spend a moment more with some thoughts on this wonderful person known as the Lord Jesus Christ. It seems to me that in this book God reveals the ultimate vindication of the Messiah (the Christ, the Anointed One), Jesus of Nazareth, as predicted in Psalm 2. He has set his anointed on his holy hill and he will reign as King. He is King of Kings. His people can experience his rule here and now, and they will see it expressed in a time to come. Come with me and see John expressing his worship of the Lord for all that he is and has done for us. He writes, 'I, John, am writing this to the seven churches in Asia province: All the best to you from THE GOD WHO IS, THE GOD WHO WAS, AND THE GOD ABOUT TO ARRIVE, and from the Seven Spirits assembled before his Throne, and from Jesus Christ – Loyal Witness, Firstborn from the dead, Ruler of all earthly kings. Glory and strength to Christ, who loves us, who blood-washed our sins from our lives, who made us a Kingdom, Priests for his Father, forever – and yes, he's on his way!'

John is writing to those who along with the Lord Jesus are now a kingdom and priests – that is, the churches. 'I, John, am writing this to the seven churches'. These are the people who have been freed from their sins by the precious blood of Jesus. See Verse 5, where John tells us of Jesus, 'who loves us, who blood-washed our sins from our lives'. Yes, we are his kingdom on earth today, but there is also to be a future kingdom on earth. We read of it in Chapter 11: 'A crescendo of voices in Heaven sang out, the kingdom of the world is now the Kingdom of our God and his Messiah! He will rule forever and ever!' What a wonderful message for the Lord's people! The world may appear at times to have a mighty dragon in it, and the churches seem like lambs being pursued by that dragon, but they will one day be forever with their Lord, see his face and be shepherded by him. Then nothing will harm them or cause offence forever and ever.

We need only to be reminded of the importance of revelation to realise the importance of reading this book. It is the light to show us the way through a dark, sinful world, and without it we would go hopelessly astray. As the wise man tells us in his proverb, 'If people can't see what God is doing, they stumble all over themselves; but when they attend to what he reveals, they are most blessed.' Peter confirms this in his second letter: 'The prophetic Word was confirmed to us. You'll do well to keep focusing on it. It's the one light you have in a dark time as you wait for daybreak and the rising of the Morning Star in your hearts.' This Book of Revelation is said by the Lord Jesus to be prophecy. John was told to write, 'And tell them, "Yes, I'm on my way!" Blessed be the one who keeps the words of the prophecy of this book.' The Angel continued: "Don't seal the words of the prophecy of this book; don't put it away on the shelf. Time is just about up – I give fair warning to all who hear the words of the prophecy of this book: If you add to the words of this prophecy, God will add to your life the disasters written in this book – if you subtract from the words of the book of this prophecy, God will subtract your part from the Tree of Life and the Holy City that are written in this book."

God who knows the end from the beginning has chosen to give us a selective knowledge of things that must take place. It is our responsibility to read and take to heart what he has revealed. Back in history, when God first took Israel from Egypt and gave them the privilege of being entrusted with his revelation, he said through Moses to them in Deuteronomy, 'GOD, our God, will take care of the hidden things but the revealed things are our business. It's up to us and our children to attend to all the terms in this Revelation.' The great apostle Paul knew the importance of revelation to the people of God. He prayed in Ephesians: 'I ask – ask the God of our Master, Jesus Christ, the God of glory – to make you intelligent and discerning in knowing him personally, your eyes focused and clear, so that you can see exactly what it is he is calling you to do, grasp the immensity of this glorious way of life he has for Christians, oh, the utter extravagance of his work in us who trust him – endless energy, boundless strength! All this energy issues from Christ: God raised him from death and set him on a Throne in deep heaven, in charge of running the universe, everything from galaxies to governments, no name and no power exempt from his rule. And not just for the time being, but forever. He is in charge of it all, has the final word on everything. At the centre of all this, Christ rules the church. The church, you see, is not peripheral to the world; the world is peripheral to the church. The church is Christ's body, in which he speaks and acts, by which he fills everything with his presence.'

May the Holy Spirit give us revelation that we may have our eyes focused and clear, so that we can see exactly what it is he is calling us to do. We must grasp the immensity of this glorious way of life he has for his people.

We have already observed that the revelation is given to John to send to those who have come to faith in Jesus as their saviour and who are meeting together to worship the Lord by obedience that comes from faith and works by love.

The one chosen by the Lord to write this Book of Revelation also wrote an account of the life of the Lord Jesus, including his death and resurrection. At the close of the Gospel of John he made it clear why he wrote it: 'Jesus provided far more God-revealing signs than are written down in this book. These are written down so you will believe that Jesus is the Messiah, the Son of God, and in the act of believing, have real and eternal life in the way he personally revealed it.' To have this real and eternal life we must repent of our sins and receive Jesus as our saviour. As John wrote earlier in his Gospel: 'But whoever did want him, who believed he was who he claimed and would do what he said, He made to be their true selves, their child-of-God selves.' A leading teacher asked Jesus how this was possible and Jesus said, "Take it from me: Unless a person is born from above, it's not possible to see what I'm pointing to – to God's kingdom." This is only possible by the revelation given by God. In Matthew, 'Simon

Peter said, "You're the Christ, the Messiah, the Son of the living God." Jesus came back: "God bless you, Simon, son of Jonah! You didn't get that answer out of books or from teachers. My Father in heaven, God himself, let you in on this secret of who I really am." '

At some point every true child of God who is part of his churches has come to the point the apostle Paul came to. He said in relation to their sin, 'I realize that I don't have what it takes. I can will it, but I can't do it. I decide to do good, but I don't really do it; I decide not to do bad, but then I do it anyway. My decisions, such as they are, don't result in actions. Something has gone wrong deep within me and gets the better of me every time. It happens so regularly that it's predictable. The moment I decide to do good, sin is there to trip me up. I truly delight in God's commands, but it's pretty obvious that not all of me joins in that delight. Parts of me covertly rebel, and just when I least expect it, they take charge. I've tried everything and nothing helps. I'm at the end of my rope. Is there no one who can do anything for me? Isn't that the real question? The answer, thank God, is that Jesus Christ can and does. He acted to set things right in this life of contradictions where I want to serve God with all my heart and mind, but am pulled by the influence of sin to do something totally different.' The action that God took in Jesus was the death of the Sinless One on the Cross for the sinners who could not save themselves.

Oh yes, thank God! We can say to all who ask, "What must I do to be saved?" The Bible says whoever calls out to Jesus for forgiveness, believing that he died for their sins, will be saved.

Allow me to make a further point as we come to what the Lord Jesus had to say to the churches in the next chapter. Revelation has a very subjective application to the individual and to the churches. For example, the Lord may reveal to the church that is convinced it is alive that in fact it is dead. Or he may tell the church convinced its orthodoxy is evidence of the love they have for the Lord that they have lost their first love and that without love it all counts for nothing in the eyes of the Lord. We should therefore live as this book exhorts us to in the light of the fact that Jesus is coming again. As Peter wrote in his first letter: 'So roll up your sleeves, put your mind in gear, be totally ready to receive the gift that's coming when Jesus arrives. Don't lazily slip back into those old grooves of evil, doing just what you feel like doing. You didn't know any better then; you do now.'

We also note that John tells us he recorded for us all he saw: 'And John told everything he saw: God's Word – the witness of Jesus Christ'. The Lord Jesus by his angel gave John the things that must take place in the form of symbolic visions. What he saw contains the message of the Lord for us. Sometimes he is told what to write, but mainly he wrote what he saw.

Again at the beginning of Chapter 1 we note the things John is shown are about to happen: 'A revealing of Jesus, the Messiah. God gave it to make plain to his servants what is about to happen." Looking back now over the 2,000 years since John wrote down for us what he saw, we can see that some of the things recorded in the Book of Revelation took place during the fall of the Roman Empire and have been taking place ever since. However, the pattern seems to be that they will become increasingly global and get more intense.

The first thing I ever saw on the television was the coronation of our present queen. We were told the coronation was about to happen, and we saw things begin to happen as the procession began to move, but it was some hours before the Queen was finally crowned. The things John saw in his visions began to happen not long after he saw them; they are still happening and events will continue to unfold until there is a new heaven and a new earth and the Lord will dwell with his people for eternity.

We must take heed of what John has recorded of all that he saw, because it is the word of God brought by Jesus to John to write down for us, and we are promised that reading it and taking it to heart will result in blessings for us. God's word can become a beam of light on our dark path, so that it may be said of us that we keep the commandments of God and the faith of Jesus. We have a hope that is a certain hope; we have a priest who is interceding for us.

Jesus is our hope, and we see him in the Book of Revelation as the King Priest addressing each of his churches. It is an exhortation from the Lord Jesus to be ready for his coming again, and this wonderful hope keeps us going on with the Lord. Our hope is in the grace of God. The first reference to this hope is in Ezra, where we read, 'Shecaniah son of Jehiel of the family of Elam, acting as spokesman, said to Ezra: "We betrayed our God by marrying foreign wives from the people around here. But all is not lost; there is still hope for Israel." ' When the apostle Paul was reasoning out the gospel in his letter to the Romans, he made it clear that the hope of Israel is not in trying to keep the law, but in faith in the finished work of the Lord Jesus on the Cross. Jesus and his atoning sacrifice on the Cross is our hope. Allow me to close this chapter with a quotation from the writer to the Hebrews: 'And now I want each of you to extend that same intensity toward a full-bodied hope, and keep at it till the finish.' And I wish to add three quotations from the apostle Paul: "The lines of purpose in your lives never grow slack, tightly tied as they are to your future in heaven, kept taut by hope. The Message is as true among you today as when you first heard it. It doesn't diminish or weaken over time." And, "With that kind of hope to excite us, nothing holds us back." And finally, "So speak encouraging words to one another. Build up hope so you'll all be together in this, no one left out, no one left behind. I know you're already doing this; just keep on doing it."

Chapter 2

JESUS IN THE CHURCHES
Revelation 2 and 3

We come now to the first vision that John saw. He tells us how it happened and when it happened. It was on a Sunday morning, and he became aware that he was 'in the Spirit' in a special way. He heard a voice behind him that in volume was like the noise of a great waterfall. He could not only hear the noise; he could feel it. He turned to see where the voice was coming from. Turning, he saw seven candlesticks and walking among the candlesticks he saw, in symbolic form, a man whom John understood to be the Messiah, Jesus of Nazareth.

He had known Jesus for three years and was convinced Jesus was the Messiah. John wrote to one group of Christians about his experience of Jesus: 'From the very first day, we were there, taking it all in – we heard it with our own ears, saw it with our own eyes, verified it with our own hands. The Word of Life appeared right before our eyes; we saw it happen! And now we're telling you in most sober prose that what we witnessed was, incredibly, this: The infinite Life of God himself took shape before us. We saw it, we heard it, and now we're telling you so you can experience it along with us, this experience of communion with the Father and his Son, Jesus Christ.'

John had no doubt who Jesus was, and he tells us this was who he saw by using the title for the Messiah that Jesus often used himself: Son of Man. John was one of twelve men chosen to be special apostles – eye witnesses of Jesus's ministry, death, resurrection and ascension. This same Jesus said to John, "Write what you see in a book and send it to seven churches that are in Asia." John was again to be an eye witness and to write down all he saw. He recorded it for us in this Book of Revelation.

The Son of Man John had seen going to the right hand of the majesty on high was now standing before John in a form that symbolized his office as the King Priest among the churches. He wore the garment of a priest down to his feet with a golden breastplate. John then looked at the head of the one before him and noted that his hair and beard were white as snow and his eyes were piercing through the gleam of the white from the head and beard with light shafts of fire. As John fell at the feet of the one before him, he noted that Jesus's feet had the glow of bronze in a furnace. However, unlike the image seen by Nebuchadnezzar, the one seen by John here is alive. All the symbolism is of one from whom great glory, majesty and awesome power is emanating – and he is walking and talking. He is alive. This one then dictated to John what he was to write to the churches.

Rather than look at each letter, I invite you to consider that the message to the churches may be expressed in the words of the Lord Jesus to the church in Laodicea: "Look at me. I stand at the door. I knock. If you hear me call and open the door, I'll come right in and sit down to supper with you."

The first exhortation is to "Look at me." The first part of the message to the churches is to keep their eyes on Jesus, who, as the writer to the Hebrews tells us, "both began and finished this race we're in. Study how he did it. Because he never lost sight of where he was headed – that exhilarating finish in and with God – he could put up with anything along the way: cross, shame, whatever. And now he's there, in the place of honour, right alongside God." The Lord Jesus told

John to tell the churches that is where all who are passionately faithful will be.

I invite you to give a little thought to this exhortation. "Look." It is not just a glance; it is the look of one examining something important. Everything about him is significant to us as we seek to live for him through the things that must take place before he comes again. The "Look at me" is important. We may get carried away with ourselves if we look at ourselves and compare ourselves with some other church. The church that knows how to look to the Lord for an accurate assessment of itself is a blessed church.

The place angels play in the purposes of God in relation to the churches is an important one, and there is teaching in this book as well as the Book of Acts on this subject; but we need to keep our eyes on Jesus if we are to understand the things that must take place before the end comes.

Many of us reading this book will have gleaned wonderful messages and teaching from each of these letters by going through each one in the order they are given to us. As I have already said, it is not my intention to try to give a text-by-text study of this book, so I would like now to describe each of the symbols of Jesus John saw. They are mentioned at the beginning of each letter: who Jesus is, what Jesus has done and is doing, and the authority that Jesus exercises.

Who Jesus is: John is told to write that the one speaking to the churches is the 'First and Final One'. He is the First in that he existed before any created thing came into being. All that is created was created by him. Genesis 1 teaches us that the word of the Lord has creative power. He said, "Let there be light," and there was light. Jesus proved who he is when here on earth he used his power to create through his word. He raised the dead, gave sight to those born blind, restored the withered arm of a man, and healed someone miles away simply by speaking the word of healing. He is also the Final One, having finished once for all time the work of salvation when he died and rose again; there is no one else we are looking for. There is no other name in which we can find salvation. No one becomes a child of God except through Jesus.

He is the Son of God – another title for the Messiah and an expression of the nature of the Lord. He is God the Son in a unique relationship between the Father, Son and Holy Spirit. He could say, "I and the Father are one. If you have seen me, you have seen the Father." We are taught in this Book of Revelation that angels are involved in the relationship between the Lord and his people, but Jesus is superior to all the angels. He is the Son of God; they are the servants of God. We are looking to Jesus the Son of God, not to angels or any other beings. Like the apostle Peter, we can say, "There is no one else we can go to, Lord. It is you who has the words of life." When John is shown the Throne room of heaven, the worship is to the One on the Throne and to the Lamb. We read, 'To the One on the Throne! To the Lamb! The blessing, the honour, the glory, the strength, For age after age after age." While here on earth, Jesus made his relationship to God clear; the Jews understood what he was saying and they tried to stone him for it. John tells us in his Gospel, 'The Jews were now not only out to expose him; they were out to kill him. Not only was he breaking the Sabbath, but he was calling God his own Father, putting himself on a level with God.'

John is told to write to the church in Philadelphia: 'These are the words of him who is holy and true.' The Lord is by nature holy; we are all by nature unholy. Our human nature is sinful; but Jesus, even though he is a man with a human soul, is without sin. He could be tempted in all points, just like us, but his nature is holy and there is nothing of sin in him to respond to those temptations. His response was to reject the temptations with "Get behind me, Satan." And he is truth; there is nothing false in him at all. He is truth, and everything is tested by him. The things that must take place are taking place even though the world is deceived by the antichrist. Those who are looking to Jesus will not be deceived because truth will expose lies. This is why that passionate first-love relationship with Jesus is so important. If we lose that, we are in danger of losing the light of our testimony for the Lord. Our eyes are on him, like the lover in the Song of Songs has her eyes on her lover. By looking to Jesus, the people of God will be kept holy and true through all the things that must take place. Jesus himself is the lamp to our feet and the light to our path. He is our light through this dark world.

Jesus is also the Amen. He only did what he saw the Father do and said what he heard the Father say. He is the one in whom all the promises of God are fulfilled. All the scriptures point to him and are about him. He is therefore the faithful and true witness to all that God has revealed to the human race. No matter how deceitful the coming world powers that Satan will bring into the world may be, they will not deceive us if we keep our eyes on Jesus. We will know they are not of God. The local churches cannot be led astray by false prophets or immoral practices if they maintain their passionate relationship with Jesus.

John is also told to write to the church in Laodicea that Jesus is 'the ruler of God's creation'. The writer to the Hebrews tells us, 'He holds everything together by what he says – powerful words!' So when, among the things that must take place, the world begins to fall apart (as is shown later on in the Book of Revelation), we must remember that nothing happens but it is allowed by the One Who Holds Everything Together. He must first give the word from the Throne. The people of God have the wonderful comfort of knowing that the One Who Holds Everything Together will always do what is right because it is his nature to do so. Just as he created all things by his powerful word, he also holds all things together by that same powerful creative word.

The symbols that John saw in Chapter 1, and with which

he was told to begin each letter, not only show us who Jesus is, but they also show us what he has done and is doing. He is not only the One Who Was; he is also the One Who Is.

First let's look at what he has done: 'Died and came to life again'. This is in the past – the never-to-be-repeated work of the Lord Jesus on the Cross. Once Jesus had demonstrated to the disciples who he is, he began to tell them he must die. He taught them that it was for this very purpose that he had come. We are taught in the scripture that the death of Jesus was an atoning sacrifice for our sin. It not only made forgiveness possible, but it also freed us from the power of sin. It was a redeeming sacrifice that freed us from Satan and the power of sin. It was also a reconciling sacrifice. It brought us into a right relationship with God, and it made communion with a holy and righteous God possible for sinners who have been brought to faith in Jesus. We can therefore say, "I was saved 2,000 years ago, when the Lord Jesus died on the Cross and rose again, but I came into a realization of it at a point in time." Our salvation is an historical fact. The apostle Paul said that if we are justified by the death of Jesus, we are also glorified by that same death and nothing else at all. The work he began he will complete.

What is Jesus doing now? He is walking among the churches – or, as we have it in the Message translation, he is 'striding through' the churches. He is the King Priest inspecting his kingdom; he has the stride of the sovereign among his people. What a wonderful comfort it is to the people of God to know that the King is among us! He is on the battleground, not away in some far-off land. He is right in the thick of the things that must take place, so that none whom the Father has given to him will be lost.

The next symbol shows us the weapon our King uses for the battle we are engaged in: 'the sharp, double-edged sword'. The writer of the letter to the Hebrews tells us that the word of God is the sharp two-edged sword that brings conviction to the sinner and conversion to the Lord. We may see in the symbolism of the sword coming from the mouth of the one John saw that it is the word in the Spirit that gives life, not the dead letter of the page. Everything in the symbolism of the Book of Revelation has pulsating life about it. We shall see this more and more as we go through the book. Our God is a life-giving spirit, speaking and active today. To the church in Thyatira John is told to say that the one sending this letter to them had 'eyes like blazing fire'. He is now engaged in keeping his eye upon his people and seeing into the innermost being of each one. Yes, he loves us and his desire is to bring out into the light what needs dealing with. God knows everything about us. As Paul teaches us in his Roman letter, we have all sinned, and because of sin we are under the cloud of the righteous judgement of God, but 'With the arrival of Jesus, the Messiah, that fateful dilemma is resolved. Those who enter into Christ's being-here-for-us no longer have to live under a continuous, low-lying black cloud. A new power is in operation. The Spirit of life in Christ, like a strong wind, has magnificently cleared the air, freeing you from a fated lifetime of brutal tyranny at the hands of sin and death.' There is now no condemnation for those who are in Christ Jesus. God, who sees all, now sees us in Jesus.

To the church in Thyatira he also was told to say that the one writing to them has the symbolic sign of 'standing on feet of furnace-fired bronze'. He is standing in the fire with his people when they go through the fire, as he was with the three friends of Daniel. He can stand the fire and come out pure, and so can those who are passionately faithful to their Lord. They have 'washed their robes, and made them white in the blood of the Lamb'. They have been to the Cross in repentance and faith to see that their sins have gone forever in the eyes of God.

To the church in Philadelphia John is told to say that Jesus is the one who opens doors for them. 'I have placed before you an open door that no-one can shut.' There are many powerful things going to happen – things that must take place – but no-one will be able to close any door that the Lord has opened. He is still walking among the churches and for them he is opening doors they could not open themselves. How many of those of us reading these words can think of doors that in our weakness we could never have opened, but which the grace of God has opened for us!

The churches for their comfort were shown who Jesus is, what Jesus had done and what authority he has. More was shown as the revelations continued, but in the letter to Ephesus John described a vision in which Jesus 'holds the seven stars in his right hand'. We have been told that these stars are the angels of the churches. They are held in the right hand of the Lord, who has them completely under his control. He is above the angels. The writer of the letter to the Hebrews tells us that these angels are sent to aid those who will receive salvation: "Isn't it obvious that all angels are sent to help out with those lined up to receive salvation," and they are in the hand of Jesus. What a comfort to know that we have been shepherded into the fold of God by the Good Shepherd and his angels! They guard and keep us, and, whatever must take place, nothing will be able to pluck us out of his hand.

John is told to write to the church in Sardis that the one who is writing to them has authority over the gracious work and enabling power of the Holy Spirit. The number seven, as we will see, symbolizes completeness or wholeness. The symbolism here seems to teach us that all the gifts and fruit of the Spirit come to us by the Spirit through the Lord Jesus, our living saviour. God is at work to bring about, in us and through us, his good pleasing and perfect will. This he does by his Spirit through the authority given to Jesus. Hence Peter could say to a crippled man, "I don't have a nickel to my name, but what I do have, I give you: In the name of Jesus Christ of Nazareth, walk!" And he walked. Because Jesus is 'holding the Seven Spirits of God in one hand', as the churches face the things that must take place they know that greater is he who is in you than he who is in the world.

John is told to write to the church in Philadelphia that the one who has all authority over the angels and the Holy Spirit is the one who also has the authority that was promised to one who would be a descendant of King David of Israel: 'who holds the key of David'. This is what was promised to the Messiah. Jesus has this authority and is still using it today. "All authority", he could say to the disciples, "has been given to me in heaven and on earth. You go into the world and remember I am with you with all this authority." Globalization of authority is becoming an increasing reality before our eyes, but Jesus tells us, "Be of good cheer. I have overcome the world, and in me you too will have the grace to passionately stand faithfully with me." This wonderful book shows in many symbolic ways that the people of God have an amazing sense of security through all the changing scenes of life. The One Who Has All Authority told John to write down for his people for all time, 'Look at me.'

He then told John to tell them, "I stand at the door. I knock." It must remain a constant challenge for each local church to ask if they are aware of the presence of Jesus in the meetings. We know that Jesus said, "When two or three of you are together because of me, you can be sure that I'll be there." How much aware of him are we? "I am here," he is saying, "but am I in the centre of the meeting? You know all about me – who I am and what I have done and am still doing with all authority – but am I King Priest in your meeting together?" We would all, I am sure, agree that the presence of Jesus will keep us through all that is happening and the things that must take place before Jesus comes again. So to each of the churches John is told to write some aspect of the person or function of the Lord Jesus according to what he saw of Jesus in the first visions. The living Lord Jesus, who is in the churches, holds the angels of the churches in his right hand. He is the beginning and the end of all things. He was there when all things were created by him, and he will be there at the end. The end of all things is not in the hands of man; it is in the hands of Jesus, our living saviour. He is the power and life in the word of God that is sharper than any two-edged sword. The effectiveness of the word of God is in and through the Lord Jesus. His eyes pierce all hidden places and his feet can progress over all situations. Nothing is hidden from him and nothing will prevent the progress of his good pleasing and perfect will. He has the keys to all doors. Nothing is forbidden to him. He can even enter Hades, putting in or taking out whom he will. He is faithful at all times. He will do right and see that righteousness is done. This is the one calling for the attention of the church. He can open all doors, yet he calls for those within the church who hear his voice to open the door. He will not impose. When he was on earth and cast out demons into pigs, they asked him to leave. They wanted to close the door to their town to him, and he let them. He wept over Jerusalem. He would have entered in and blessed them, but they would not welcome him. They closed the door. Would you agree that it is possible for a group of the Lord's people meeting together in his name to close the door to his living, speaking influence in the church? From this message it seems that it is possible to turn our eyes on to other things or people and away from the Lord, even as we meet in his name. We need always to have the attitude 'self on the cross and Christ upon the throne'.

Consider with me the things the Lord mentioned to these churches that had taken their eyes off him and were in danger of closing the door to him. First he speaks of his displeasure regarding their engagement in so much activity that it had become routine rather than part of their relationship with himself. We may even feel we cannot take the time to be alone and listen to his word – to be in communion with him –

because we are so busy doing good work for him. I recall one occasion, as I began to read my Bible, with a concordance, a dictionary and a commentary on the passage I was reading, I felt the Holy Spirit say, "This is not about me at all, is it? This is about you studying the scripture and preaching next Sunday. It should be about communion with me, which means listening to me." I put all the books away, and for several days I came to the Lord to listen to him. The result was that I had a wonderful time of refreshing.

At about that time, one of the older members of the church said to me after I had preached one Sunday morning and evening, "I think, Brother Tony, you are experiencing personal revival."

The Lord Jesus said to Peter in a penetrating conversation after breakfast one morning, "Simon, son of John, do you love me?"

O, may the Lord never have to say to us, "You walked away from your first love."

Secondly, the Lord Jesus warns against the temptation to be hesitant in doing whatever he tells us (in action or word) because of what others may do to us. The Lord says to us, "Fear nothing in the things you're about to suffer – but stay on guard! Fear nothing!" I can recall at one church being worried about the response of a group of people within the church to the message I was preaching. I held back on saying what I knew had to be said and I lost my peace with the Lord.

Thirdly, the Lord Jesus clearly warns against being too tolerant of opposition to the Lord's will: "Why do you indulge them? And why do you put up with them? Enough! Don't give in to them." In the light of the challenges that are coming upon the whole earth we may do well to remember the words of the Lord to his people of old: if you cannot run with men, how will you run with horses?

Fourthly, be on guard against taking away from the Cross.

There is, in the eyes of the All-Seeing One, a religion that is 'cross-denying, self-indulging religion'. Do we need any explanation of what these words mean? We might consider that the self-righteous who seek their own righteousness by the law are cross-denying.

Fifthly, the message of the Lord was to avoid burying our heads in the sand – or rather, "you pull the covers back over your head and sleep on, oblivious to God". O, how comfortable we can become in our sleepy, cosy, religiously busy lives! We become oblivious to the signs of the times that God gives to us in this prophetic revelation. We too can, with the church at Laodicea, become 'not cold, nor hot'. Not only was the Lord not able to eat with them in fellowship, but they made him 'want to vomit'. "Keep looking at me," he appeals to them. "Turn to me from these other things. It is me that will keep you through all that is recorded in this book. If you maintain your love for me, your love will mean you will not do anything against my will. You will know what is my good pleasing and perfect will."

If you will repent and 'open the door' to Jesus, he said, "I'll come right in and sit down to supper with you" – as he did in the upper room after his resurrection. He will point out what is good and praiseworthy in the church and what needs to be changed.

The Lord Jesus is seen by John in Revelations 1 among the churches as their King Priest. In him, as Paul writes, 'Everything that we have – right thinking and right living, a clean slate and a fresh start – comes from God by way of Jesus Christ.' John burst out into praise in Chapter 1 of the Book of Revelation with the declaration, 'and from Jesus Christ – Loyal Witness, Firstborn from the dead, Ruler of all earthly kings. Glory and strength to Christ, who loves us, who blood-washed our sins from our lives, who made us a Kingdom, Priests for his Father, forever – and yes, he's on his way!'

Allow me to close this chapter by asking if you have been to Jesus for the cleansing power of his precious blood, shed on the Cross for our sins. It is the only way to be cleansed; and, having been cleansed, it is by the power of the Cross and our testimony to it that we can stand for the Lord through all that is said to have to happen before he comes again. As John writes for us later in this book, of those who were faithful to Jesus against Satan, "They defeated him through the blood of the Lamb and the bold word of their witness. They weren't in love with themselves; they were willing to die for Christ."

I would like to share a thought that came to me while writing this chapter. John was told to write what he saw of things that must take place, but before he saw those things he had to write what Jesus saw in the churches. Maybe we should give first priority to what the Lord sees in the church, and then we should look at the signs of the times. The churches would of course have confirmation of the authenticity of what John was writing because they would know the truth of what Jesus revealed about their church. We, like Nathaniel when Jesus said, "I saw you sitting under the fig tree," will respond, "You are the Son of God, the King of Israel!"

One more thought on the fact that the communication is in the form of letters: it is the personal nature of a letter that makes this relationship with the Lord so precious to us. Yes, the revelation the Lord gives to us contains laws, rules and instructions, but it is always in the context of a personal relationship. It is that personal relationship of the Lord with his people that is brought out right at the beginning of the Book of Revelation in these seven letters.

In this revelation Israel and the Jewish people are mentioned several times, and we need the help of the Lord as we think on these things. At this point, in relation to the Book of Revelation, I would like to note the place in which John saw his visions. The place was an island off the coast of Turkey, and the churches were all on the trade route on the west coast of Turkey. I find it interesting that the last book of the Bible comes to us from a land other than Israel and is written to a people other than the Jewish people, or Israel as a nation. It is to largely Gentile churches, in a Gentile land that is a bridge from the East to the West. We see a reason for this in the seventh chapter of this book.

Jesus is alive and ministering to his churches, because the churches have a vital role to play in the purposes of God. Jesus said, "Let me tell you why you are here. You're here to be salt-seasoning that brings out the God-flavours of this earth. If you lose your saltiness, how will people taste godliness?" They are, as Paul teaches us to be, bastions of truth. What a fitting symbol is chosen for the churches: a lamp stand, which is the carrier or upholder of the Light of the World – that is, Jesus.

Chapter 3

THE HOLY SPIRIT IN THE CHURCHES
Revelation 2 and 3

Many years ago I had the privilege of serving the Lord in Morocco for a short time. A local man was giving me hospitality when there was a knock at the gate to the yard in front of the house.

The friend shouted out, "Who is it?" He would not answer the door until he recognized the voice of the one knocking.

The issue of recognizing the voice of the Lord has always been a challenge to me. "My sheep", Jesus said on one occasion, "know my voice and will respond to my voice." One of the wonderful facts about being a child of God is the personal relationship each one of us has with the Lord. Each of the letters reminds us that the Lord is not just speaking to the church as a whole but to any of the members of the church who hear his voice.

Allow me to ask the question, is the challenge for us getting a local church to agree on how we listen to the voice of the Holy Spirit? It has been my joy over fifty years now to have fellowship with almost all the forms of worship that the Lord's people practise. I have never been in a group where we have all been able to agree on this matter of hearing what the Lord is saying. Broadly speaking, the meeting usually ends up in two parties, one wanting a Bible study and the other a prayer meeting. Both are wonderful in themselves, but the important thing, it seems to me, is that the group comes to an agreement and is able to act on it. Otherwise it becomes a wait-and-see-what-happens approach or a compromise of opinions. Surely the fact that the Lord Jesus asked John to write seven times, urging different churches to listen to the Spirit, at least reminds us that each church is not like any other group of people trying to decide what to do about a given issue. There must be a place, when faced with an issue, for asking the question, what does the Lord say about this issue now, today, to us? When there is clear instruction in the scripture the matter is easy, but I have found that getting people to distinguish between what the texts of the Bible say and their interpretation or application is more difficult than it seems. Please be patient and allow me one more thought here. The old saying, 'If a thing is working don't try to change it,' does not seem to apply to the churches. Some of these churches thought things were working wonderfully well, but the voice of the Lord came and said, "You are deceived by your own self-satisfaction. I am not at all happy with things the way they are." How we recognize that voice has to be agreed on if division is to be avoided when the Lord begins to change things to the way he wants them.

A friend of mine, having preached at a local church, was speaking to an elderly member who said he had been there for several decades (I have forgotten just how many).

My friend said, "You must have seen some changes in that time."

He said, "Yes, I have, and I resisted every one of them!"

Amusing? I wonder.

It is because of my past experience that I approach this chapter with a lot more trepidation than I have the others in the book so far. I attended a meeting the other day where a brother took as his text, 'The amazing grace of the Master, Jesus Christ, the extravagant love of God, the intimate friendship of the Holy Spirit, be with all of you.' He spoke eloquently on the grace and love of God and hardly mentioned the Holy Spirit. There came to my mind that this experience of intimate friendship in the Holy Spirit is one I do not talk about much and may find difficult to put into words. The words *intimate* and *passionate* do not come easily to mind in expressing my relationship with the Lord. I feel the same is true of the exhortation of the Lord Jesus to the seven churches in the Book of Revelation to listen to the Spirit and what he has to say to the churches. If we express our understanding or experience of this, we may find many differing explanations and experiences, but there can be no doubt about the importance of it in the mind of the Lord Jesus. It is part of the message of the head of the church to his churches as we come to the close of the written word of God.

I am not equipped to try to present the understanding or experience of the churches over the past generations. We have much recorded evidence, but that is not my brief for this book. However, may I invite you to ask yourself what has been your experience and the experience of your churches regarding intimate friendship or fellowship in the Spirit? What has been your experience and your church's experience of listening to the Spirit?

I invite you now to come with me and look at the fourteen times the Spirit (capital S) is mentioned in the Book of Revelation. The first occasion is in the first chapter, when John describes his experience on that Sunday morning: 'I was in the Spirit, praying.' Clearly John was aware that this was not just something he was doing with his own intellect or imagination while praying. He felt himself enveloped by the Holy Spirit, and as a result what he has recorded for us in the Book of Revelation is not what John himself chose to write. It is what he was told to write by the Lord Jesus through his angel. This was no normal Sunday morning time of worship for John. This experience he tells us was 'in the Spirit'. I think he used that term to convey to us that this was not a normal Sunday morning experience for even John, the apostle whom Jesus loved. We may not expect to have the vision of Jesus that John had, and certainly not the commission given to him in the vision, but I suspect many will be able to testify to times when the presence of the Lord has been felt in a special way. May we learn to listen especially carefully on such occasions, because the Lord Jesus said clearly to each of the churches that if they had ears to hear, it was vital they obeyed in faith out of love for him and then they would inherit the promises he made to them.

Having looked at the first reference we note that half of the fourteen times that the Spirit (capital S) is mentioned occur when the Lord Jesus is exhorting the seven churches to listen to the Spirit.

In the Message translation the translators have expressed the exhortation of the Lord as follows: "Are your ears awake? Listen. Listen to the Wind Words, the Spirit blowing through the churches."

This is not an easy translation for me to relate to. I am still at heart a King James Version man, but I am finding the Message Bible refreshing and helpful. In the Message translation they have expressed for us the sense that the experience has mystery about it. Now, many of my friends will throw their hands up in horror at the very use of the word *mystery*. They are convinced that guidance today comes solely by the objective knowledge of scripture. Well, I agree that we need all the knowledge we can get of the scripture. I do, however, often remind these friends that on several issues they do not agree on what the scripture actually says. Allow me to use an example. Many years ago now, the leadership team, of which I was a part, realized that several people in the congregation were divorced. We wondered what our response should be if any wanted to remarry in the church building. Well, after three months or so there were, as I recall, three different opinions as to what the scripture taught about marriage, divorce and remarriage. To this day some still disagree on this issue. Why did we not know how to listen to what the Spirit was saying to us as a church? Most of the team at that time believed we should not even ask that question. They believe all that the Spirit has to say to us today is already recorded in the scripture. Well, as I have said, I am not capable of writing down the results of years of discussions and studies on the gifts of the Spirit and listening to the Spirit. It would not profit at this point in the book to simply recount them. I began to seek the Lord towards the end of the 1950s, which was around the time of the beginning of the charismatic movement, and in the early sixties I had three years' training at Swansea Bible College. I have myself known the direct guidance of the Holy Spirit on several occasions, and I often speak of the voice of the Holy Spirit speaking to me, but I have never been accepted by the charismatic movement as being a charismatic. Nor have I been accepted by those who say they are reformed as being of their persuasion on this matter of listening to the Spirit. Looking back, I can see that in all the churches where I have had the privilege of worshipping the Lord we have never been able to agree as a group on experiencing the Spirit speaking to the church.

The symbolism chosen by the Lord for the Holy Spirit descending upon Jesus is a dove. His nature is dovelike; he does not impose himself; he can be resisted, quenched or grieved about by the people of God.

We must move on now to the next time the Spirit is mentioned. I bring these comments to a close with the quotation from the Message translation again: "Are your ears awake? Listen. Listen to the Wind Words, the Spirit blowing through the churches."

In the fourth chapter of the Book of Revelation John is shown, in symbolic vision, the awesome authority of the Spirit coming direct from the Throne in heaven. John tells us, 'Lightning flash and thunder crash pulsed from the Throne. Seven fire-blazing torches fronted the Throne (these are the Sevenfold Spirit of God). It is from the Throne of God in heaven that the complete (sevenfold) authority of the Holy Spirit comes. He, as the New Testament teaches us, is the third person of the Holy Trinity, one with the Father and the Son, of whom it is said, 'In the beginning they said, "Let us make man."' ' Listen to what the Holy Spirit has to say, for his word has all the authority of the Throne of God behind it. Surely, then, we must be clear in our minds how we are to hear what he has to say to us.

In Chapter 11 of the Book of Revelation John is told by the Lord Jesus to record for us a vision of two witnesses in Jerusalem who have a powerful ministry and because of it are eventually put to death. The world rejoices because of this – their bodies are left for people to see and rejoice over – but then suddenly they are standing on their feet again alive. John tells what happened: 'Then, after three and a half days, the Living Spirit of God will enter them – they're on their feet! – and all those gloating spectators will be scared to death.' It is the Holy Spirit that brings about their resurrection, and afterwards they are seen to rise up to heaven. The power of the Holy Spirit is seen here – the power to bring life out of death. We can read of this in the teaching of the apostle Paul. Of the death and resurrection of the Lord Jesus, he wrote, 'His descent from David roots him in history; his unique identity as Son of God was shown by the Spirit when Jesus was raised from the dead, setting him apart as the Messiah, our Master.' In another place, when teaching us what we have been given as the children of God, Paul teaches us that the power that is at work in us is the power that raised Jesus from the dead. It is by the power of the Holy Spirit, which raised Jesus from the dead, that we are born again to become children of God.

John continues in the Book of Revelation to record for us

what he was told to record by the Angel of the Lord Jesus. He tells us in Chapter 14 that the Holy Spirit bears witness to what was said from heaven. 'I heard a voice out of Heaven, "Write this: Blessed are those who die in the Master from now on; how blessed to die that way!" "Yes," said the Spirit, "and blessed rest from their hard, hard work. None of what they've done is wasted; God blesses them for it all in the end." '

Here we have the witness of the Holy Spirit to the word of God. We may say that we experience this when we are reading the written word of God. There is a witness within us that says amen to what we are reading. It is the Holy Spirit witnessing to our spirit, and we believe and by faith are pleasing to God. It is the Spirit speaking, and because we are listening our response is obedience that comes from faith and works by love.

John tells us several times in the Book of Revelation that he was picked up and taken by the Spirit to see remarkable things. These seem to be unique experiences given to John for recording in this unique book. I can write nothing on this, other than to comment on the wonderful grace of God that told John to record these things for us.

We will conclude our following of John's references to the Spirit in the Book of Revelation by looking at the final one, in Chapter 20. "Come!" say the Spirit and the Bride. Whoever hears, echo. "Come! Is anyone thirsty? Come! All who will, come and drink, Drink freely of the Water of Life!" It is the appeal of the Lord Jesus through the churches by the Spirit throughout the whole of time from his ascension until he comes again. The New Testament teaches us, "God isn't late with his promise as some measure lateness. He is restraining himself on account of you, holding back the End because he doesn't want anyone lost."

On this matter of listening to the Spirit allow me a few quotations from the Book of Acts, relating the experience of the Lord's people. 'The Spirit told Philip, "Climb into the chariot." ' And, 'Peter, lost in thought, didn't hear them, so the Spirit whispered to him, "Three men are knocking at the door looking for you." ' There is also the experience of the leaders of the church in Antioch: 'One day as they were worshipping God – they were also fasting as they waited for guidance – the Holy Spirit spoke: "Take Barnabas and Saul and commission them for the work I have called them to do." '

And so John's account to the churches of his first vision comes to a close with, "Are your ears awake? Listen. Listen to the Wind Words, the Spirit blowing through the churches."

Chapter 4

JESUS IN THE THRONE ROOM OF HEAVEN
Revelation 4 and 5

On our journey through the Book of Revelation we have seen that the message is Jesus is alive and is with his churches, related to them by John, through the Holy Spirit and the scripture. God gave John the command to record what he would see of the things that must take place right up to the end of this world and the creating of a new heaven and earth.

John is now given another vision, and this time it is of heaven and the amazing splendour of all the glory of God. Coming to this vision we may well remind ourselves that the one we are seeing here on the Throne ruling over the whole universe – the subject of the praises of the whole universe – is the one the Lord Jesus teaches us to call our Heavenly Father.

Many have noted that the first vision ends with a closed door; the Lord Jesus is on the outside of his church, and, to our surprise, it is a church that has all the appearance of being a prosperous, successful church. We may well pause for a moment here and note that it is possible for the Lord's people to become so taken up with their service for the Lord that their communion with him is lost. A church might be doing what they believe to be the will of God, but it is what they want to do for him, it is not walking with him. In one of his parables the Lord Jesus told the people about two brothers and the way they related to their father. The one brother –

the older of the two – worked hard on the farm and all the father's business, yet it is clear he had no real relationship with his father. His heart was further away from the father's than the younger brother had been in a faraway country. Like Israel of old we can resist the Spirit, insisting we will serve the Lord but in our own way and according to our own understanding. Isaiah is told to preach of Israel that, "they rebelled, and vexed his Holy Spirit: therefore he was turned to be their enemy, and he fought against them". It was repentance and faith as well as the forgiveness of his father that brought the younger boy back into a passionate relationship with his father.

As the first vision ended John saw another door, and this one was open. It opened into heaven. Again we may think of the parable and the return of the younger brother. He found that the door to the father's house was wide open and the father was on his way to escort him into the house with great celebration. We are left in no doubt in this vision that heaven is a place of great celebration. Jesus said to the disciples that they would one day be with him where he was going. Now John is given a vision of where Jesus is. He is right at the centre of the Throne in heaven, with all the occupants of heaven worshipping in great celebration.

I have chosen as a text to guide us through this vision a verse in Chapter 5: 'I saw a scroll in the right hand of the One Seated on the Throne. It was written on both sides, fastened with seven seals.' John had been shown that the churches are the Kingdom of God on earth and their function is that of priests. The Bible teaches us that the priests were to be governed by the word of God and to govern the people by that same word. Ezra is a great example of that teaching. 'Ezra had committed himself to studying the Revelation of GOD, to living it, and to teaching Israel to live its truths and ways.' It is the importance of the word of God and the testimony of Jesus that John is about to be shown.

John was shown, in the Throne room of heaven, that God has chosen to give a written record of his revelation for the human race of his good pleasing and perfect will. I would for this vision like to revert to my preacher role and to put the contents of the vision under three headings: 'The Word', 'The Worthy One', and 'The Worshippers'. I am also tempted to put in, as a fourth heading, 'The Weeping One'.

John was told to record what he saw. What he saw has a message for the people of God. John was shown that all things that must take place are governed from the Throne on which sits the Creator and Redeemer of his people and the whole of the universe. Entering heaven in an attitude of worship, in the Spirit, John saw a throne and one seated on it bathed in brilliant colours that resembled the flame of a fire – an amber light with a deep-red centre all shimmering like a roaring fire with a strong draught blowing through it. The scene is one of life; our God is a life-giving Spirit, not something speechless and unable to act. There is a sense also of awesomeness, for our God is a consuming fire, as the writer of the letter to the Hebrews teaches us: 'God himself is Fire that will purge away all sin from among his people.' John was able to look on all this light because it was bathed in a green hue that mellowed it for his eyes. When Jesus appeared to Saul on the Damascus road, even a part of this light blinded Saul for a time. John tells us that the effect of all this light was to give the appearance of a rainbow encircling the whole of the Throne and the one seated on it. What comfort this would have given to those struggling, persecuted churches! The rainbow would have reminded them of the faithfulness of God. The Lord gave a rainbow for Noah to see after the Flood with the promise 'I will never do this again;' and even though the human race has provoked the Lord ever since, he has been faithful to his promise.

John recorded for us that he saw in heaven a symbolic representation of all the redeemed people of God; and the representatives of the redeemed creation were groaning, worshipping the one on the Throne, their faithful great creator. Many more symbols of the awesomeness of the presence of the Lord are given. These were experienced previously by Israel and recorded for us in the Old Testament: lightning, thunder, then a sea like glass that brings a calm sense of wonder – full worship, worship full of wonder.

Having observed all this splendour and majesty, John's attention was drawn to the book or scroll in the right hand of the one on the Throne. There has been discussion about which part of the word of God this scroll represents. It is not an issue for those in need of comfort and guidance as they face persecution and struggles within the churches. It is sufficient to take it that it represents the written word of God. It is in the Lord's right hand. He has government over what is recorded by the inspiration of the Holy Spirit. There are secret things that belong to the Lord our God, but the things he has revealed are for us and our children. The Lord has made it clear that he has not recorded for us everything to do with himself and his purposes, but he has given to us sufficient for us to have faith that what he has promised he is well able also to do.

John noted that the scroll was full, having writing on both sides of it. This teaches us that with the Book of Revelation the word of God is completed. There is nothing else to add and nothing must ever be taken from it. John was told to make that clear in this last book of the Bible. 'If you subtract from the words of the book of this prophecy, God will subtract your part from the Tree of Life and the Holy City that are written in this book.' Here in the Throne room of heaven there is a symbolic reminder that we must keep the word of God central to our lives if we are to be victorious through all the changing situations of life; and the churches need to keep the word of God central to their worship and witness for the Lord. The writer of the letter to the Hebrews teaches us that God 'means what he says. What he says goes. His powerful Word is sharp as a surgeon's scalpel, cutting through everything, whether doubt or defence, laying us open to listen and obey.' The church needs to listen to the Spirit through the word of God.

It is clear right throughout the Book of Revelation that it is always the Lord that takes the initiative. John did not decide to write this book; he was arrested by the Spirit and told to write it by the Lord Jesus. John never asked questions; he was asked questions, but he always declined to answer, asking rather to be given the answer. That should of course be our attitude as we read the word of God. The Lord himself tells us that it is the humble he teaches, but John was affected by what he saw and we are told that on this occasion he wept when he was shown that no one from the heavenly beings or on earth can open up the scroll. The people chosen to minister the word of God are themselves burdened by the word they have to minister. Paul received an amazing revelation about the relationship between the Jew and Gentile. He tells us that this revelation came about because his heart was affected with deep anguish as he went around preaching: 'At the same time, you need to know that I carry with me at all times a huge sorrow. It's an enormous pain deep within me, and I'm never free of it. I'm not exaggerating –Christ and the Holy Spirit are my witnesses.' And later he writes, 'Believe me, friends, all I want for Israel is what's best for Israel: salvation, nothing less. I want it with all my heart and pray to God for it all the time.' John knew the churches needed what was in that scroll, and he wept uncontrollably when it seemed it would remain a closed book.

The secrets of the Lord are given to those who have a heart for them and are moved by them; it is not just an objective academic knowledge. One prophet wrote that he decided to quit preaching because no one really wanted to hear what he was saying, and he tells us, 'I could not keep quiet; it became like a flame in my heart bursting to get out into the open.' John, we will find, had a similar experience in another vision a little later on.

In this present vision the word of God was closed and sealed; the things that must take place (which John had been told he was to be shown) were still hidden. No one could open it up for him to see. Then an elder comforted him and he was told, "There is one who will open it up for you." He is the one who is 'the Lion from Tribe Judah, the Root of David's Tree'. John knew this must be Jesus, the Messiah, the one he had seen in the first vision walking among the churches as the King Priest. So he looked to see where this one was in the Throne room, and when he saw him it was as the Lamb of God that had been slain and lives again. What a wonderful thing for the Lord to show himself here in the Throne room, not in the symbolism of the King Priest, but as he was introduced by John the Baptist. "Here he is, God's Passover Lamb!" is the way John and Andrew were first introduced to Jesus. The Lamb of God, slain on the Cross for the sins of the human race and risen again to life to prove the sacrifice was acceptable, secured eternal salvation for those who come to repentance and faith in him. This is the one who will open up the scroll, as he opened up the scriptures to the two on the Emmaus road. The Messiah had to suffer, he told them, and he opened up the scripture to their minds. They understood that the Cross is the key to the opening-up of the scripture. John is shown here that not only is the Cross the key to all that is past, but it is the key to all the things that must take place until Jesus comes again. Not only to the churches on earth, but here too in the Throne room of heaven, God shows us in this symbolic vision that the Lord Jesus Christ, his death on the Cross and his resurrection are the key to all the revelations given to us in his word. That is why the apostle Paul writes to the church in Corinth, 'You'll remember, friends, that when I first came to you to let you in on God's master stroke, I didn't try to impress you with polished speeches and the latest philosophy. I deliberately kept it plain and simple: first Jesus and who he is; then Jesus and what he did – Jesus crucified.'

Jesus alone is the worthy one. As the worshippers express in this vision that John was shown, "Worthy! Take the scroll, open its seals. Slain! Paying in blood, you bought men and women, Bought them back from all over the earth, Bought them back for God." This revelation will show us that he will 'take the power, the wealth, the wisdom, the strength! Take the honour, the glory, the blessing!' John is shown that, eventually, 'every creature in Heaven and earth, in underworld and sea, join in, all voices in all places, singing: To the One on the Throne! To the Lamb! The blessing, the honour, the glory, the strength, For age after age after age.'

Jesus through the scripture by the Spirit is the lamp to the feet of the churches and light to their path.

In the Bible we are taught that God has chosen that the revelation he has for mankind is written down for them. It is not everything about God and all that God has planned, but it is all that he has chosen to give us to see. For example, in Deuteronomy Moses is told to record for the people, 'GOD, our God, will take care of the hidden things but the revealed things are our business. It's up to us and our children to attend to all the terms in this Revelation.' Daniel was told to seal up some things that they might not be known, and John is told not to record some things he heard. What we have been given is sufficient for us to have faith in God – to believe he is able to do what he has said he will do.

As we read what John has recorded for us here, may I invite you to remember that we cannot hope to understand what is recorded for us in the Book of Revelation without a knowledge of what God has revealed for us in the whole of the Bible – Old and New Testaments. If we take note of what is recorded, we will know that the David written of here is

King David of Israel. We do well to note this because we will not be able to forget this ancient people of God as we read through what John saw and recorded for us in the Book of Revelation. I ask you to also observe as we go through this revelation that this people known as Israel have some part to play in the things that must take place before Jesus comes again and the new heaven and earth are brought into being.

To the churches the Lord has shown through this symbolic vision that he is on the Throne and in control. He knows the end from the beginning and he gives insights into things that must take place before the new heaven and earth are brought into being. We shall see later the wonderful revelation that the people of God shall be with the Lord for eternity, where there is no possibility of sin ever again entering the experience of his people. The Lord Jesus on the last occasion he was with his followers before the Cross said, "my parting gift to you. Peace." A very real sense of wholesome well-being – that is the peace I have. The Lord said this as he was facing the Cross. It is not the peace the world gives, which is dependent on circumstances. The Lord gave this revelation of the things that must take place knowing that he can give peace to the hearts of his people even when they know these things must happen.

To know this peace, the Bible teaches us, we must come to a personal faith in Jesus. The door to heaven is open, even if the door to the church is closed as it was at the end of Chapter 3. The apostle Paul teaches us we must call on the name of the Lord Jesus for forgiveness of sin and receive him as Lord of our lives if we personally are to experience this peace. In his letter to the Romans he writes, 'By entering through faith into what God has always wanted to do for us – set us right with him, make us fit for him – we have it all together with God because of our Master Jesus. And that's not all: We throw open our doors to God and discover at the same moment that he has already thrown open his door to us. We find ourselves standing where we always hoped we might stand – out in the wide open spaces of God's grace and glory, standing tall and shouting our praise.'

It is Jesus who has given us the Book of Revelation, in which John has recorded for us what he was shown by Jesus, our wonderful Saviour. John tells us at the beginning that those who are blessed are not only the ones who read or hear the words of this book; it is those who take them to heart that are blessed. With that in mind, allow me to remind you of the words that God gave to Ezekiel in relation to the nation of Israel, who knew the word of God but did not take it to heart: "As for you, son of man, you've become quite the talk of the town. Your people meet on street corners and in front of their houses and say, 'Let's go hear the latest news from GOD.' They show up, as people tend to do, and sit in your company. They listen to you speak, but don't do a thing you say. They flatter you with compliments, but all they care about is making money and getting ahead."

May our gracious Lord grant us grace to listen to the Spirit and follow the advice of Mary, the mother of Jesus: "Whatever he tells you, do it."

Chapter 5

JESUS AND THE NATIONS
Revelation 6

I was just about to begin Chapter 5 of this book, which will cover the next vision in the Book of Revelation. I was having breakfast and listening to the BBC World Service news. One young politician said of an emerging political movement, there is an animal in our country that at the moment is stalking quietly, but the time will come when it will spring into action. The fact that he used an animal as a symbol of an event taking place in his country brought to my mind the use of animals in the Book of Revelation to symbolize the things that must take place before the coming-again of Jesus. From Revelation 6 to 8, John sees seven horses.

The Lord Jesus who is the King Priest to his churches and the Worthy One in the Throne room in heaven begins to open the seals on the revelation of the things that must take place. I wonder if, like me, you have noticed the constant speaking and movement that takes place in the Book of Revelation. Everything is living and responding to what is said, and heaven is responding to the prayers of the people of God. Like Jacob's dream there is constant movement from heaven to earth and earth to heaven.

As we are led into the vision, we may consider for a moment the words translated in the Message: "I'll show you what happens next," and, in the New International Version, "I will show you what must take place after this." In the Authorized Version it is translated as, "I will show thee things which must be hereafter." It seems to me, having looked at a variety of interpretations of these words, that John is being told here of things that would begin to happen from that time on and continue to happen right up to the end of this present world. It certainly seems to be the case, looking back now over the 2,000 years from when John was given this revelation. The things we are shown in the opening of the seals have been taking place and are beginning to become more global and intense as we move on towards the end. That is the way I have come to understand what John is shown. It makes the whole of the message of the Book of Revelation timeless and applicable to every generation that reads it.

In this vision John is shown an overview of what will be the history of the world right up to the end of this world as we now know it. We do well to remember that this world will one day come to an end. The Bible teaches us this in many places. For example, Paul in his letter to the Corinthians teaches that the general resurrection will take place at the time of the end, and Daniel was told to close what he had written because it was for the time of the end. "This is a confidential report, Daniel, for your eyes and ears only. Keep it secret. Put the book under lock and key until the end. In the interim there is going to be a lot of frantic running around, trying to figure out what's going on." There is no need for that frantic running around now. The Lord Jesus in the Book of Revelation tells us the things that must take place before the end comes.

We are to look now at the opening of six of the seals. Each opening brings a loud command from one of the animals around the Throne. The time has come and the Throne has commanded that action be taken. This is a comforting realization for every child of God because they know that the judge of all the earth will do right. He only acts in judgement when the sins of the people have become self-destructive, as in the cases of the Flood and Sodom and Gomorrah.

John saw a conqueror who was able to be victorious over all

around him. If there was peace it was because he had the rule of a dictator over the people. The Romans certainly had this and so have many world powers since, and we rejoice in the knowledge that from the first the gospel has been going throughout the world, bringing people under the Lordship of Jesus. It seems to me that the white horse may symbolize bloodless rule over peoples and countries. Many people have been conquered without war or bloodshed by the use of material gain or ideology (which may appear to be pure and righteous) as well as by the gospel. It could be said that the West was conquered by the gospel, in that the governing powers were largely influenced by it. That influence has been getting less and less over the last century. Now the emerging world powers do not have that same influence of the gospel in their cultures.

Then another command and another horse: this one is able to make mankind fight one another in terrible wars. In the vision there is much bloodshed, peace is taken from the earth, and war is the dominant characteristic of the experience of the human race. How true this has been! Throughout the world, empires have collapsed and dictatorships have crumbled. Those previously forced to live in peace with one another have expressed nationalism and ethnic demands that have often led to wars. In 2008, wars seem to be on the increase. Each war not only affects the nations fighting; the whole of the global system is affected. I think especially of Israel and the Middle East; peace has evaded the attempts of so many to try to bring peace to that region.

In the vision, another horse comes out when the third seal is opened. This time he has the ability to cause shortages on the earth. Food becomes very expensive, but wine and oil are readily available. We are all very aware now of famines and shortages in so many parts of the world. We can see them on the television and the awful consequences of them. As with the wars, these famines are becoming more global. I heard a report that the grain stores of the world are now lower than they have been for many years, and the situation is being made worse by a financial crisis that is affecting the whole of the world. There have been shortages before, and inflation out of control before, but the Lord Jesus is saying that these things will continue to be part of the history of the world and they will get worse in the end time.

When the fourth seal was opened John noticed that the horse this time was sickly white. Many will die and many others will suffer spiritual torments. The fact that John is shown death – 'and Hell was close on its heels' – may symbolize that many will die having not accepted the gospel of the Lord Jesus. We will see a little later the prediction that many will cry for the rocks to bury them to hide from the righteous judgement of God. Some would rather be buried alive than repent and be saved – for such, Paul teaches us, after death is the judgement and hell. There is a sober awesomeness about what the Bible teaches us, and we have a responsibility to share it.

The human race may say, "There is no God. I will stamp him out of my mind," but the consciences of those people will not be at rest. These are the tribulations that are to come upon mankind as a result of their decision to follow sin and self-satisfaction in spite of the opportunity they have been given to turn to God in repentance and faith.

Having recorded for us the spiritual suffering after death in a place called Hell, John was shown that the children of God will also be persecuted by the people who will not repent of their sin. Like Cain, who could not stand Abel and his right relationship with God through the sacrifice acceptable to God, those who do not accept the sacrifice made by Jesus for our sin will persecute and put to death those who do repent through faith in the Lord Jesus.

John was then shown the souls of those who had died for their faith in Jesus. They are with God, and their presence there is crying out like the blood of Abel for justice to be done. They are comforted by the Lord, who is the God of all comfort. They are told there will be a right time for unrepentant sin to reap what it has sown. This right time is one of the things revealed in this book. We do not know the time, but we are told that even though all these things have happened in the past and are happening now, there is coming a time called the Great Trouble or Great Tribulation when these things will get more intense and be all over the world.

The sixth seal was removed by the Lord Jesus, and John was aware of a great earthquake affecting the whole earth. Even the heavenly bodies seemed to be affected. Mankind, John tells us, will be thrown into 'pandemonium, everyone and his dog running for cover – kings, princes, generals, rich and strong, along with every commoner, slave or free. They hide in mountain caves and rocky dens, calling out to mountains and rocks, "Refuge! Hide us from the One Seated on the Throne and the wrath of the Lamb! The great Day of their wrath has come – who can stand it?" '

The terrible thing is that all the people will be aware that this is the righteous judgement of God that they have been expecting. The atheists will not convince mankind there is no God. When the end comes they will know that God is and everyone will have to give an account of themselves to him. Even after the tribulation that is experienced in this world, there is still a judgement to come, as the Lord Jesus taught us when he said that Sodom and Gomorrah still have to stand before the Judgement Throne of God. In Matthew 11 Jesus said to the unrepentant cities of his day, "And Capernaum! With all your peacock strutting, you are going to end up in the abyss. If the people of Sodom had had your chances, the city would still be around. At Judgement Day they'll get off easy compared to you."

As we close this chapter, may I remind you that the Bible teaches us there will be, at the end, a final judgement and we will not all end up in the same place. In his letter to the Thessalonians, Paul writes that the final judgement will take place when Jesus comes again. It will be a glorious time for those who have come to faith in him according to the light given to them in the Bible, but it will be a terrible time for those who have rejected God and the light he has given to the human race in the Bible. This is how the words of Paul in his letter to the Thessalonians are translated in the Message: 'You need to know, friends, that thanking God over and over for you is not only a pleasure; it's a must. We have to do it. Your faith is growing phenomenally; your love for each other is developing wonderfully. Why, it's only right that we give thanks. We're so proud of you; you're so steady and determined in your faith despite all the hard times that have come down on you. We tell everyone we meet in the churches all about you. All this trouble is a clear sign that God has decided to make you fit for the kingdom. You're suffering now, but justice is on the way. When the Master Jesus appears out of heaven in a blaze of fire with his strong angels, he'll even up the score by settling accounts with those who gave you such a bad time. His coming will be the break we've been waiting for. Those who refuse to know God and refuse to obey the Message will pay for what they've done. Eternal exile from the presence of the Master and his splendid power is their sentence. But on that very same day when he comes, he will be exalted by his followers and celebrated by all who believe – and all because you believed what we told you.'

So when we see these things happening, remember our redemption is drawing nearer. The delay is because the Lord who does not want any to perish is waiting until sin has run its full course and there is no more opportunity of delay.

Jesus showed John, who has recorded it for us, the fact that in the eyes of God there are only two groups of people on earth: those who are his people by repentance and faith in Jesus, and those who are not his people. There are those who choose to go against his revealed will and even fight against him, trying to the very end to suppress the knowledge of God in their conscience, and those for whom Jesus is a lamp to their feet and a light to their path through life. Jesus himself is the Way, the Truth, the Life.

Chapter 6

UNTIL
Revelation 7

Jesus had shown John what would be the history of this world as we now know it, including what would happen right through to the end of time and into eternity. John also saw that the people of God would be secure for eternity with the Lord, under his guidance and provision, enjoying all he has prepared for them.

Now, in this seventh chapter of the Book of Revelation, we have an example of how the Lord Jesus at certain points focuses in on some special point for John to see and record for us.

There are two wonderful truths in the continuing vision that John records for us here.

He saw four angels standing 'with a firm grip on the four winds so no wind would blow on earth or sea, not even rustle a tree.' The firm grip of the angels is a great comfort to the people of God. We are taught in other places in the Bible that God weighs everything he allows into the life of his people, and his angels have a firm grip on everything that must take place.

A great angel is sent to these four angels telling them to continue holding back the winds of judgement *until* they are given the command to release them. The Lord Jesus is showing his churches here that the timing of all the things that must take place is in the hands of the one upon the Throne in heaven. The angels with the authority to release these things are bound. They are not able to take any initiative. Even the things that happened to the Lord Jesus while he was here on earth could not happen until the time came for them to happen. John tells us in his Gospel that Jesus said, "I'm telling you all this ahead of time so that when it happens you will believe that I am who I say I am." And later on, 'Jesus said these things. Then, raising his eyes in prayer, he said: Father, it's time. Display the bright splendour of your Son So the Son in turn may show your bright splendour.'

The Book of Revelation confirms this time and again, telling us that events begin by a command from the Throne in heaven. We are told that before the events being held back can take place the great angel has something he must do, "until I've sealed the servants of our God on their foreheads!" Now with a sense of excitement we note that these servants of God are said to be of Israel. (Remember we noted before that this nation of Israel chosen by him to bring the Messiah into the world is not finished with.)

John tells us, 'I heard the count of those who were sealed: 144,000! They were sealed out of every Tribe of Israel.' We took note a little while ago that we need to have an understanding of God's dealings with Israel if we are to understand what is being shown us in the Book of Revelation. We saw previously that one of the confirming signs that Jesus is the Messiah is the fact that he was born a descendant of David, the King of Israel. This is not about his deity but about his office as Messiah. Now again we are presented with Israel, and this time the servants of God are from every tribe of that nation. We have been told that the Book of Revelation is made up of symbolic visions, and we are told the meaning of some of the symbolism, but it also has material facts in it. There were seven churches in the seven towns mentioned in the first two chapters. There was and still is a nation called Israel, and this nation is throughout the scripture set apart by God. All the other nations are said to be Gentile nations. It seems that this nation of people, Israel, has within it those who are the sealed servants of God. They will be protected against the intensifying of the things that must happen on the earth. In his letter to the Romans, Paul refers to them as the Israel within Israel.

Now the churches who read this prophecy first were, like us, aware that the Word of God teaches us that the only way to become children of God now is by being saved. We know that one of the big questions in the early church was what about Israel now that God had shown that salvation is open to all nations? Everyone who calls on the name of the Lord will be saved – Jew or Gentile. But only those who call will be saved – Jew or Gentile. The New Testament, and especially the books of Romans and Galatians, teach us that in Jesus Christ there is no difference. Jew and Gentile become one in him. In Romans 9 through to the end of Chapter 11, Paul, under the inspiration of the Holy Spirit, teaches us that there is a number chosen by the God of Gentiles and Jews who will be saved. This word *until* is used by Paul when he is teaching us that the majority of the Israelites had been cut off from God because they refused to accept Jesus as the Messiah and Saviour. They preferred to go on under the law rather than accept their need and turn to God in repentance and faith. In their place, Gentiles in large numbers have turned to God through faith in Jesus. Paul tells us this is only *until* all the Gentiles have come into the family of God; and then all Israel will be saved.

In this amazing vision given to John after the sealing of the servants of God from the tribes of Israel, John recorded for us that he saw in heaven before the Throne an innumerable company from every nation. The full number of the Gentiles was in, and all Israel that is to be saved are sealed. All hell may be let loose, but not one of the Lord's people will be lost – Jew or Gentile. The order of the events that must take place and the timing of them are in the Father's hands and not a sparrow falls to the ground without his knowledge. How much more valuable are we, his people, for whom he gave his one and only Son to die on the Cross as an atoning sacrifice for our sin? Jesus paid a redemption price, setting us free from the consequences of sin and enabling us to be reconciled with God.

Allow me to address myself to you, dear reader, at this point. Are you saved? Do you have assurance that you are a child of God? Please consider what the Bible teaches us: we all need to be saved because we have all sinned. It is not a matter of feeling myself to be a sinner; God says I am a sinner. It is my sin that separates me from a holy and righteous God. Because the consequence of sin is death, every sinner must die for their own sins. That is why Jesus, the Sinless One, had to die for us. He need not have died, but he chose to take our place and take our death for us. John, who had the responsibility of recording what he saw in the Book of Revelation, also wrote in his Gospel about Jesus and those who believed in him. 'But whoever did want him, who believed he was who he claimed and would do what he said, He made to be their true selves, their child-of-God selves. These are the God-begotten.' These are the ones who are saved of Jews and Gentiles, and they will be forever with the Lord, as the Book of Revelation shows us.

I would like at this point to share a thought that came to me some time ago as I was praying for the situation in Israel between the Jews and Palestinians. I believe God still has a purpose for the Jews and Israel, the land promised to Abraham and his descendants, but this does not make a Jewish person a child of God. They too need to be saved by faith in Jesus and his death on the Cross. The apostle Peter stated that there is no name given under heaven by which we may be saved other than the name of Jesus. Therefore, if a

Palestinian man believed and called on Jesus for salvation, he would be saved and become a child of God. On the other hand, if a Jewish man rejected Jesus and said, "I will not have this man to rule over me," he would not be a child of God even though he was living in the land promised to Abraham and his descendants through Isaac. This is the clear teaching of Paul in his letter to the Galatians. Writing to the Christians in Galatia, he issued a strong warning about going back under the law and thinking they could save themselves with a self-righteousness that denies the atonement made by Jesus on the Cross. He writes, "Isn't it clear, friends, that you, like Isaac, are children of promise? In the days of Hagar and Sarah, the child who came from faithless connivance (Ishmael) harassed the child who came – empowered by the Spirit – from the faithful promise (Isaac). Isn't it clear that the harassment you are now experiencing from the Jerusalem heretics follows that old pattern?"

Natural birth for Jew or Gentile will never make a person a child of God. You must be born again by the Spirit of God through faith in Jesus. This is the clear Gospel message for Jew or Gentile.

We have now been shown that some of the things that must happen began to happen in the time of the Roman Empire. They have been happening ever since. There are some things still to come in the future; they will be global and much more severe than anything so far, but the people of God, both Jew and Gentile, who have come to faith in Jesus will be kept by the grace of God. Ultimately they will be with Jesus for eternity.

Chapter 7

PRAYER
Revelation 8 and 9

John is made aware that the occupants of heaven realize something momentous is about to happen. The whole of heaven is a place of activity and noise like the sound, John tells us, of water falling over a waterfall. God sometimes comes to his people as a still small voice, and at other times as a rushing mighty wind. Part of the adventure of walking with the Lord is that we never know which it will be.

John saw the angels preparing to go forth with the final judgements of God on the people of the earth. Then John was shown a wonderful scene: it is the mingling of the prayers of the people of God with the worship of the hosts in heaven. The prayers are brought before the Throne in a golden censer (gold is symbolic of deity). The prayers are brought in the name of Jesus the Son of God and presented on a golden altar. The Cross of the Lord Jesus is the altar through which we approach God. Our prayers are to the Father through the Son by the Holy Spirit. They are about God and his purposes revealed in his word. John sees the angel take fire from the altar and throw it to the earth in response to the prayers of his people. The time has come to answer the prayers of his people so that righteous judgement will be seen to be done. Daniel saw from the word of God that the time had come for the Jews to go back to the Promised Land. Having seen the will of God in the scriptures, Daniel gave himself to prayer for the revealed will of God to be done on earth as it is in heaven.

John recorded for us the terrible effects of these judgements as the human race reaps what it has sown. A third of the produce of the land is burned up and becomes unproductive, like a forest that has been set on fire. Then a third of the sea becomes so polluted that a third of the life in the sea dies and a third of the merchant ships and pleasure ships are sunk. Things get worse as John sees a third of the drinking water become polluted and undrinkable, causing the death of some. Added to these disasters is the fact that a third of the light from the heavenly lights – and therefore a third of the day – is lost.

John was shown that even while all this is taking place God will still have a voice declaring his word. An angel flying through the air symbolizes that nothing can hinder the progress of the spread of the word of God. No mountain is too high nor valley too low to stop the progress of this message to all the nations of the earth.

John then saw things begin to get worse for the people of the earth. They have lost a third of the natural provision of the earth, and, while they try to cope with this, terrible spiritual influences come upon them. They will not repent and turn to God, so they are open to the evil influences of Satan. In symbolic form John sees the release of evil spirits among the people. The people have chosen evil over good and now they reap the fruits of it. These evil forces are very powerful and beguiling, and, even though it brings suffering, people continue to submit to their influence. The people have no ability to control or overcome them, and people begin to long for death rather than continuing to experience the torment they are in. It is amazing that people will endure all kinds of material loss, physical suffering and even emotional torment rather than repenting and turning to God.

These evil spirits are not allowed to affect the environment because that has been seen to by God himself. God does not directly inflict these torments on people; they bring them on themselves by the choices they make. Eventually the time comes for the final judgements to begin; God can hold back the judgements no longer. The result is that a third of the people of the earth die in the events that take place, but still the remainder will not call on the name of the Lord Jesus for salvation. There will still be a witness for the Lord in the preaching of his word, and there will also be the fact that the people of God will be seen to not suffer in the same way as the people of the world. The two kingdoms will be clearly divided: those under the lordship of Jesus, and those who have chosen the kingdoms of the world in selfishness and self-will, worshipping Satan and evil spirits often represented by idols and images.

In the eighth and ninth chapters of the Book of Revelation, having become accustomed to the noise of loud voices and the constant movement taking place, John then tells us that he became aware of a stillness and silence. I can recall the feeling I had while standing outside during the eclipse of the sun some years ago. As the final stage of the eclipse took place, and the sun was fully covered, there was a strange feeling of stillness and silence. Even the birds stopped singing. It seems that John had a similar experience at this point in the revelation. The Lord Jesus is about to open the seventh seal and the whole of heaven becomes silent, aware that something momentous is about to take place.

The angels waiting to respond to the Lord's will are given seven trumpets so that all will be aware of what is about to happen. The events are to be heralded by trumpet blasts. Heaven will know when these things are to happen. No one in heaven will be unaware when the time comes for action. There will also be those on earth who will know, as Daniel in his day knew, the time has come for the Jews to go back to the land of Israel. The Lord said to Israel through Amos, "The fact is, GOD, the Master, does nothing without first telling his prophets the whole story." The events about to happen will be trumpeted in heaven.

John was then shown also that the prayers of the people of God will be involved in what is about to take place. They are prayers prayed by the people of God, informed by his word. We have a wonderful example of this in Daniel: when he saw the time had come for God to take action, he gave himself to prayer for the Lord to honour his word. He tells us, 'Darius, son of Ahasuerus, born a Mede, became king over the land of Babylon. In the first year of his reign, I, Daniel, was meditating on the Scriptures that gave, according to the Word of GOD to the prophet Jeremiah, the number of years that Jerusalem had to lie in ruins, namely, seventy. I turned to the Master God, asking for an answer – praying earnestly, fasting from meals, wearing rough penitential burlap, and kneeling in the ashes. I poured out my heart, baring my soul to GOD, my God: "O Master, great and august God. You never waver in your covenant commitment, never give up on those who love you and do what you say." '

What an amazing thing this is! The people of God, praying the Lord's will be done on earth as in heaven and that righteousness will be seen to be done for all the evil that has taken place by the hands of the sinful human race, will have their prayers answered at just the right time.

The churches will find much encouragement to pray from the Book of Revelation. Follow with me, please, the references to prayer in that book.

The first reference to prayer is in Chapter 1, where John tells us, 'It was Sunday and I was in the Spirit, praying. I heard a loud voice behind me, trumpet-clear and piercing.' Many times in the record of the experiences of the apostles in the Book of Acts we are told movements of God began when they were praying. We could all give some testimony of prayer putting us in the right frame of mind for receiving from the Lord. We could also think of Peter in prayer when he was given the vision to open the door to the Gentiles. Paul tells us that the revelation given to him and recorded for us in Romans 9: 10–11 came out of a heart's desire and prayers to God for the salvation of Israel. We are not told John was in prayer for the churches to which the Book of Revelation is addressed, but it would not be a surprise to us to discover they were in his prayers that Sunday morning. We could testify to times when we have been praying for a situation and, while in prayer, a passage of scripture has come to us, as from the Lord, speaking about the situation. The very first meeting together of the apostles after the ascension of the Lord Jesus was a prayer meeting.

The next reference to prayer in the Book of Revelation is in Chapter 5: 'The moment he took the scroll, the Four Animals and Twenty-four Elders fell down and worshipped the Lamb. Each had a harp and each had a bowl, a gold bowl filled with incense, the prayers of God's holy people.' What an amazing insight this is to the offering of our prayers before the Throne in heaven by the worshipping angels! We do of course notice the words 'God's holy people'. These would be very daunting words to us, knowing ourselves as we do, if it were not for the fact that we are taught in the gospel that we are made holy in the Lord Jesus Christ. That is why when we pray we pray in his name. It is his holiness that is accepted by God as being the holiness of all who come to Jesus in faith. Our faith is in the Lord Jesus, not in ourselves. We can only ascend the hill of the Lord with clean hands and pure hearts through the boldness that the precious blood of Jesus gives to us. Every time we approach the Lord in prayer it is with the attitude, nothing in my hands I bring; I come absolutely dependent on the Cross, knowing that if I ask anything in the name of Jesus it will be presented before the Father in heaven. Would you agree that this thought should arouse sober thought on how and what we pray for?

In Chapter 6 of the Book of Revelation we have the prayers of those who have been put to death because of their faith in Jesus and their testimony that Jesus is Lord. The Roman Caesar demanded all Roman subjects declare once a year that Caesar is lord. The Christians could not do that; they declared that Jesus is Lord, and many were put to death for that testimony. John is told to tell the churches that he saw in this vision the continued prayers of those who had been martyred. He tells us they 'cried out in loud prayers, "How long, Strong God, Holy and True? How long before you step in and avenge our murders?" ' Among them is the first one put to death for his faith. We are told in Genesis that the Lord said to Cain, "What have you done! The voice of your brother's blood is calling to me from the ground." How noble is the exercise of prayer – our prayers mingled with the prayers of martyrs and presented by angels before the Throne of God!

The reference to prayer in Chapter 8 of the Book of Revelation teaches us that all these prayers presented to God, who is in eternity, are before him not as past, present and future but as one whole. There will come a point when God will say it is enough and will respond. We are told, 'Then another Angel, carrying a gold censer, came and stood at the Altar. He was given a great quantity of incense so that he could offer up the prayers of all the holy people of God.' The response of the Throne of God to these prayers, we are told, was that an 'Angel filled the censer with fire from the Altar and heaved it to earth. It set off thunders, voices, lightning, and an earthquake.' The response from the Lord to the prayers of his people had similar phenomena to when the Lord came down on Mount Sinai to speak to Moses. John tells us, 'It set off thunders, voices, lightning, and an earthquake.' This is direct intervention by God on a global scale. 'A third of the earth was scorched, a third of the trees, and every blade of green grass – burned to a crisp.' At the same time a third of the sea will become polluted and a third of the heavenly lights will be darkened. Eventually a third of the human race will be affected, and the human race will be reduced by a third. No wonder in John's vision heaven went silent as it became aware the time had come for these awesome events to take place. This stage will be so awesome, in fact, that it will be limited to a relatively short period of time. The Lord takes no delight in the suffering of people. When judgement has to take place it is swift and short but final and irresistible.

I wonder if, like me, you are thinking at this point of all the comment there is in the news about global shortages and environmental issues. We do not know God's exact timetable, but we must surely observe the signs of the times that we are living in and voice to our relatives and friends that these things are foretold in the Bible. Sadly we have to note that John tells us that even though the human race is aware that these things are not just natural happenings – they are from God – still they will not repent. The Book of Revelation shows us that those who live through these things and are aware that they are from God still refuse to repent. It is not a passive indifference; they refuse to repent. They will not change their self-indulgent lifestyle. They 'went on their merry way – didn't change their way of life, didn't quit worshipping demons, didn't quit centring their lives around lumps of gold and silver and brass, hunks of stone and wood that couldn't see or hear or move. There wasn't a sign of a change of heart. They plunged right on in their murderous, occult, promiscuous, and thieving ways.'

At this point in the Book of Revelation the human race has experienced world powers dominating nations, wars, famines, disease and torment of soul. A third of the world's resources are gone, along with a third of the light and a third of the population, yet still they prefer to worship anything other than the true and living God – the one who is the God of Abraham, Isaac and Jacob, the God and Father of our Lord Jesus Christ.

The Book of Revelation shows us that the result is lawlessness and excess of every kind, but the people of God are exhorted to keep on praying and witnessing that by all means some might be saved.

The Lord will keep his people through it all, and his people will continue to be a witness for the Lord. He is not willing that any should perish in the final judgement, but he is just; the judge of all the earth must do right. We shall see in the next chapter what the Lord revealed to John about his witnesses.

Chapter 8

THE WITNESSES
Revelation 10 and 11

In our last chapter we were reminded that the way the Lord gives light to his people is through the proclamation of his revealed will, and the last word being proclaimed in the previous chapter was *Doom*. 'Doom! Doom! Doom to everyone left on earth! There are three more Angels about to blow their trumpets. Doom is on its way!' In this next vision it seems that the main theme is the witness of the Lord to the human race through his people that the end is now imminent.

In Chapters 10 and 11 of the Book of Revelation John has recorded for us what the Lord Jesus revealed to him about the witness his people would be to the people of the world right through to the end of time as we now know it. John was shown first the foundation of the witness of the people of God – the written word of God, which we now have in the Bible. The word of God comes from heaven and is to have influence throughout the whole earth; it is an open book for the entire human race to read and to receive instruction from as a lamp to our feet and a light to our path. John is also made aware that nothing is to be added to it; not even what John hears coming from heaven is to be written into it. He tells us, 'When the Seven Thunders spoke, I started to write it all down, but a voice from heaven said not to record what I heard.' What we have in the Bible is not something

71

concocted in the human heart. Prophecy resulted when the Holy Spirit prompted men and women to speak God's word. All who have recorded for us the scriptures must have experienced what John experienced in some way. Peter tells us that prophecy resulted when the Holy Spirit prompted men and women to speak God's word; and Paul writes, 'Every part of Scripture is God-breathed and useful one way or another – showing us truth, exposing our rebellion, correcting our mistakes, training us to live God's way.' It is God's guidebook for the direction and conduct of his people.

The posture of the angel shows us the authority with which the scripture comes to us: it is given with an oath with uplifted right hand. The angel is making clear that God is confirming his word with an oath that cannot be broken. All throughout the Bible we are told God cannot lie and that his word is 'under full warranty – never cancelled, never rescinded'. The word given by the angel is 'Time is up'. The only way the people of God will be able to know the time is up and the end is at hand is through the open word of God. This revelation given to John is the final record of the completed work of God in redemption.

John has to take this book and make it a part of him, experiencing both the sweetness and the bitterness of it. The apostle Paul writing to the Christians in Rome tells them that the gospel of God has become his gospel, and of one of the prophets we are told he came in his message to the people. To the Christians in Corinth Paul wrote that the word of God should be so much a part of them that people who will not read it should see it in their lives. Job could say, "I have made your word a priority even over my necessary food." We may note John was not given the book; he had to go to the angel and take it himself. There has to be commitment from us to take the scripture for ourselves and make it the priority of our lives. Ezra wrote his testimony for us in the words 'Ezra had committed himself to studying the Revelation of GOD, to living it, and to teaching Israel to live its truths and ways.'

John tells us that he experienced the word of God as the angel had told him he would. It was sweet to begin with but became a burden as he applied it and meditated on it. Some of the prophets who came to Israel began by saying, "This is the burden the Lord has given me." The apostle Paul on one occasion said that the burden of preaching the gospel was like the pain of giving birth to a child. There are several places in the Book of Revelation where John tells us he wept; on one occasion he wept uncontrollably.

The apostle Paul wrote in another place, 'Make sure you stay alert to these qualities of gentle kindness and ruthless severity that exist side by side in God.' Like John we have a responsibility to be faithful witnesses to the whole counsel of God without fear or favour. John was faithful in recording all that he was shown, and we may be living in an amazing time when we can see the things that must take place beginning to take place. Or at the least we can see the possibility of them taking place. Our concern for our loved ones can only be relieved by the knowledge that God is merciful and gracious and that he will do what is right. He will keep those who are his people even through the awesome things that must take place, so that one day they will be forever with the Lord in the new heaven and new earth. The rainbow in this vision is a reminder that God is faithful to his promises.

In the symbolic visions given there may be much that can be debated about times and seasons and who exactly will be on earth at the time of some of the more awesome of the events, but we may do well to remember that the first people to read the Book of Revelation were suffering from problems within the churches and from the world powers of their day. The message from Jesus is 'Keep praying!' Your prayers are being heard and brought before the Throne of God, and he will respond at exactly the right time. In order to pray according to his will, keep reading the word of God.

In a vision recorded by John in Chapter 11 of the Book of Revelation, two witnesses testify for the Lord. Their testimony is accompanied by signs and wonders to prove their message is from the true and living God, but the human race rejects these witnesses and eventually silences them by putting them to death. Then the human race rejoices by sending one another celebratory gifts. However, God raises the two witnesses to life again, and they ascend to heaven. At that time there is a great earthquake and many cry out to God. We are told this will take place in Jerusalem. 'At that moment there was a gigantic earthquake – a tenth of the city fell to ruin, seven thousand perished in the earthquake, the rest frightened to the core of their being, frightened into giving honour to the God of Heaven.' The city, I take it, is the Holy City in which John had previously been given a rod with which to measure the Temple. This is recorded earlier in Chapter 11. Isaiah was told to prophesy that one day all in Jerusalem would be holy: 'Everyone left behind in Zion, all the discards and rejects in Jerusalem, will be reclassified as "holy" – alive and therefore precious.'

I would like to ask you at this point in our journey through this wonderful Book of Revelation to consider Chapter 7 (where we have the recording by John of the servants of the Lord from the tribes of Israel being sealed) and this eleventh chapter (the city of Jerusalem being struck by an earthquake with the result of many crying out to the Lord). This may suggest to us that God will again bring the saved of Israel into play as the end-time things that must take place are taking place. Has God finished with Israel? Maybe not. Keep watching the Middle East – it may be that God will yet have a witness to the nations in that same part of the world as he chose for the drama of salvation. Jesus may return again to the land he came to the first time.

In the vision John has to take a measuring rod and measure God's Temple. Whatever view we may take about natural Israel the land and the Temple we know that when Jesus left the Temple for the last time in Jerusalem he said it was no longer the house of God. They had turned it into their house for their profit not the worship of God. Later on Paul wrote to the Christians that they were the Temple of God, and in the final vision of the Book of Revelation John sees that the city of God and the people of God are one and that there is no temple. For God himself is over his people as a temple. It is his people that God is interested in primarily. John is shown that the people of the world will be able to desecrate the things of God for a time, though God will maintain a witness for himself that will leave the people in no doubt that it is the word of God the witnesses are preaching, just as he did for Moses and Aaron in Egypt. The testimony of the witnesses will be a bright light shining out for all to see.

This time, however, will come to completion and the people of the world will be allowed to silence the witnesses just like Herod silenced John the Baptist and God removed Noah after his years of preaching by shutting the door of the Ark. God is long-suffering, not willing that any should perish, but at the right time he will execute righteous judgement. The people rejoice that the witnesses have been silenced, but God raises them up again. Though they do not say anything, their resurrection is a final witness for the Lord.

The final earthquake will take place at this point and thousands will be killed. Some, whose consciences are disturbed by the witnesses, will cry out to God. There is a distinction here between those who were convinced by the witnesses and the war party that came against the Lord. The one cried out to God; the other cursed God.

Paul wrote to the Christians that the gospel is light to some and darkness to others. It breaks the heart of some, resulting in repentance; it hardens the heart of others, who blaspheme rather than repent.

The challenge is before us: the Bible is available for us to read and be inspired to pray for all the nations of the world, but, I suggest, we should pray particularly about what is happening in the Middle East. That is where the descendants of Abraham live to this day – both those through Isaac and Jacob and those through Ishmael and Esau. If there is to be a reconciliation, it will be by the God of reconciliation through the reconciling work of Jesus on the Cross.

Could it be that through the Book of Revelation, given by God to John, we are taught that God will always have witnesses in the world from himself to the human race? Those witnesses are the churches, the Bible and the Lord Jesus by the Holy Spirit made living and personal to those who come to him in faith. Also the events taking place in the world and especially Israel and the Middle East testify to the truth contained in the Book of Revelation. We will not know in advance the exact time when things will happen, but we should be aware of any signs that do appear. For the churches who first read the Book of Revelation it must have been a great comfort to know the Creator of the heavens and earth is also the Redeemer who has all things under his control.

There is of course one who is determined to prevent the purposes of God for all his people, and we are to meet him in our next chapter.

Chapter 9

SATAN
Revelation 12 and 13

I wonder if as we progress through the Book of Revelation, you, like me, have become increasingly aware that it is not a chronological account of events.

The Lord Jesus showed John the things that would begin to take place and continue until he returns again. Then in a series of symbolic visions he showed John that it is not just people who would be involved in these things. There is a link between the unseen spiritual world and the things happening on the earth. I would like to suggest to you that the first of these visions helps us to understand that although the revelation given to John shows things that were yet to take place, it also includes things that have already taken place. For example, John sees in heaven a woman who is about to give birth to a special child. There is a dragon close by, waiting to devour the child the moment it is born, but God protects the child. He delivers it from the dragon, who then pursues the woman and tries to destroy her; but God again keeps her safe. As we read through what John has recorded for us of this vision we will look for the message the Lord has for his people as they face the way the people who do not believe will treat them.

This next series of visions covers the time from the first coming of Jesus. They take us to the second coming and through to the time when the Lord will live with his people in the new heaven and new earth that have been redeemed by the atoning sacrifice made by Jesus.

In the next vision John saw a woman who had brilliance about her like the brilliance of the sun. She was standing on the moon with twelve stars as a crown on her head. It reminds me of the dream that Joseph had when the Lord showed him he would be used by the Lord to deliver Jacob's family. It was heavenly lights that God used then for Jacob and his family acknowledging Joseph as their deliverer. The woman in the vision is crying out in the pain of delivering this child. The Bible teaches us that even though the Lord is overall God and able to protect his people, they often are allowed to enter into the pain felt by God in the process of deliverance. The apostle Paul when writing to one group of Christians tells them that when he first preached the gospel to them through which they were saved he felt such a burden in himself that he considered it to be like the pain of childbirth. In another place he speaks of sharing in the sufferings of Christ. We know, from what is recorded in the Bible, that the nation of Israel was the means through which God brought into the world the one who would be the deliverer of the people of God and indeed the whole of creation from the consequences of sin. The nation felt the pain of this exercise when through them, as Paul writes to the Romans, the Christ came into the world. The woman gives birth to the child of whom it is said that he will rule the nations; this must be the Christ promised by God, who would one day rule the nations with zero tolerance. The rule of God would be as firm and unbreakable as an iron rod. I wonder if the whole of the earthly life, death and resurrection of the Lord Jesus are passed over here because it is primarily the things that must take place that Jesus is showing the churches. One thing is for sure: the one born the Christ through the nation of Israel will one day rule as King of Kings and Lord of Lords. We also know, from the accounts given to us

in the Gospels, of the immediate suffering of the nation of
Israel in the town where Jesus was born as Herod sought to
destroy the promised Christ. Here we are shown that behind
the murder of those innocent children was Satan trying to
prevent the purposes of God from taking place. God shows
the churches that he will protect his people and provide for
them even in the desert-like experiences of the heat of
persecution.

On the way we are being taken back and forth throughout
that period to see events that must take place, but they are
not always in the order in which they will take place. I can
still recall the first time I ever saw television. It was for the
coronation of Queen Elizabeth II. It was a thrilling experience.
We were told the coronation of the Queen was about to begin,
but it took several hours from the time the procession began
to the actual coronation. Then there was the procession back
again. Often we were taken back and forward through the
procession. The things we saw were taking place at the same
time, but one camera focused on a person or a carriage, and
we would spend time on that before switching to another
camera, maybe at the back of the procession or right at the
front.

It is like that with the Book of Revelation. It is of one great
procession of the purposes of God right through to eternity,
and there are times when we are given a close-up of one
particular person or event. The Lord Jesus in this next vision
focuses on one of the main influences over the human race:
Satan. The Bible has much to teach us about this powerful
fallen angel. In this vision, John is shown what part this wicked,
lawless fallen angel would play in the events that must take
place in the remaining history of the world and the human
race as we now know it. There comes to my mind, as I think
of what John was shown here, that the first Christians were
taught these things right from the start of their faith in Jesus.
The apostle Paul was not in Thessalonica for very long, but

sometime after he had moved on he wrote to the Thessalonians, 'Don't let anyone shake you up or get you excited over some breathless report or rumoured letter from me that the day of the Master's arrival has come and gone. Don't fall for any line like that. Before that day comes, a couple of things have to happen. First, the Apostasy. Second, the debut of the Anarchist, a real dog of Satan. He'll defy and then take over every so-called god or altar. Having cleared away the opposition, he'll then set himself up in God's Temple as "God Almighty". Don't you remember me going over all this in detail when I was with you? Are your memories that short?' There are many scriptures that tell us that if the word of God is to be a lamp to our feet and a guide to our path, we need to be reminded of them again and again.

The dragon in the vision, it seems to me, reminds us that the people of God in this world are very vulnerable. As Jesus said on one occasion, "They will be like lambs surrounded by wolves," but God is their protection and not a hair of their head will be touched without him allowing it.

John was shown that the battle would not just be on earth; there would be war in heaven, but the forces of evil would be overcome by the angels of the Lord. Satan (the fallen angel) and those who followed him in the rebellion would lose the position they once held. It is certainly true that in this world the churches of the Lord Jesus are like lambs compared to the mighty power the rulers of this world have. And there will come a time when the rulers of this world will join together to try to wipe out the people of God, but greater is he that is in them than he that is in the world.

In Chapter 12 of the Book of Revelation John is shown by the Lord Jesus that behind the events that take place there is an enemy of God who will do all he can to dissuade the people of God from faithfulness in the Lord and following him in obedience that comes from faith and works by love. In the vision I suggest it is the true Israel within Israel that is seen in the woman bringing forth a child – the Lord Jesus, 'who will shepherd all nations with an iron rod. Her Son was seized and placed safely before God on his Throne.' This is certainly true of the Lord Jesus. John saw Jesus in the symbolic form of the slain lamb in the centre of the Throne in his second vision, which he recorded for us in Chapters 4 and 5 of the Book of Revelation.

The enemy is Satan. In relation to the kingdom of God on earth at this time, Satan has powerful advantages over a very vulnerable-looking people of God. The people of God are represented by a woman in labour and expecting a child at any moment. The vision of the birth of the man-child given to us certainly fits the first coming of Jesus, when Herod with all his authority and power tried to destroy Jesus as soon as he could. However, Jesus was kept until the time had come when he was to die, rise to life again and then ascend back to the right hand of the Majesty on High.

The message is that, even though the odds are all against the Lord's anointed Messiah, he will overcome Satan and will reign victorious. The church of the Old and New Testaments will be kept safe by the Lord; no one can remove the candlestick of testimony other than the Lord himself. The victory has already been won by the Lord Jesus on the Cross, and by faith in that finished work the churches will overcome Satan whether he comes as an angel of light or as a roaring lion. They will defeat 'him through the blood of the Lamb and the bold word of their witness,' because, 'They weren't in love with themselves; they were willing to die for Christ.'

Paul teaches us that it was through Israel that the Messiah, Jesus, came into the world; and the Book of Revelation teaches us that the church is his body on earth now. Satan hates both for their witness to the one who has been victorious over him, resulting in his eventual removal from the scene altogether. John was told to record for us that Satan is furious in his hatred of the Lord's people: 'Helpless with rage, the

Dragon raged at the Woman, then went off to make war with the rest of her children, the children who keep God's commands and hold firm to the witness of Jesus.' It is amazing that, right through history and today, so often the ruling authorities persecute the people of God, who because of their relationship with God are the most honest, hard-working and reliable. The world hates them because their first loyalty is to the Lord. Why? Because until we come to faith in Jesus every one of us is open to the influence of Satan. As Jesus said to the Jews who were hell-bent on putting him to death, "You are of your father the Devil and he has been a murderer from the very beginning."

In Chapter 13 of the Book of Revelation John tells us of a vision in which Satan uses two great powers against the people of God. One has all the power that the secular world can give to it. It is very swift like a leopard, and able to stand its ground with the power of a bear, devouring all before it with the mouth of a lion. The whole of the human race is brought under the control of this global power and dare not go against it. It is atheistic in nature. 'The Beast had a loud mouth, boastful and blasphemous. It could do anything it wanted for forty-two months. It yelled blasphemies against God, blasphemed his Name, blasphemed his Church . . .' This is not a religious group. Its rule is tyrannical and the Lord had John record that this is what the people wanted, and they were reaping what they had sown. 'Are you listening to this?' he writes. 'They've made their bed; now they must lie in it. Anyone marked for prison goes straight to prison; anyone pulling a sword goes down by the sword.' But, note, the people of God, chosen to be with him, 'passionately and faithfully stand their ground'. The divide in the human race between the people of God and the people who choose not to acknowledge him will become wider and clearer.

The Lord Jesus also showed John that Satan does have a second influence in the world, and this is a religious one. It has the appearance of a lamb – the counterfeit of the Lamb of God – but when this religious influence speaks it sounds more like Satan, the father of lies and murder. This influence will uphold the rule of the world governing power, encouraging people to live for themselves and their own satisfaction rather than the things of God. This religious power will be able to use magic to deceive people into thinking it has the power of God, and allegiance will be insisted upon and governed by a clear distinctive mark. We may speculate about what this might be, but the important thing is that the church learns how to discern what is of God and what is not. John is told to record for the Lord's people that they must put their "heads together and figure out the meaning of the number of the Beast. It's a human number: 666." I wonder if this is again a reminder to the churches to learn how to listen to what the Spirit is saying.

If we want an example of Satan being defeated through the discernment given by the word of God, we need only go back to the temptation of the Lord Jesus in the wilderness and learn from him to allow the Spirit to use the word of God as a lamp to our feet and a light to our path. Then our eyes will be kept on Jesus and the Cross, and we will be passionately faithful to the Lord. We will overcome by the blood of the Lamb and the word of our testimony, which is 'Jesus is Lord,' knowing that one day we shall be part of the worshipping people of God, our wonderful Creator, Redeemer.and friend.

Chapter 10

WORSHIP IN HEAVEN
Revelation 14 and 15

The Lord Jesus, having shown John the unholy trinity, 666 and the victory the people of God will have over all the wickedness and tribulation that this unholy threesome will cause to happen on earth, then gave John another vision of the worship taking place in heaven.

First John saw the Lamb and was amazed. He wrote, 'It took my breath away!' We too can testify that there are times when we are reading the scriptures and our breath is taken away by what we see as we are reading. Suddenly what we have read and known for many years becomes more real to us – often even very personal. I still thrill at the memory of the time I was studying Romans 3, a chapter I had spoken on many times. Suddenly I had an understanding of what the Cross meant to God in a way I had not seen before. John had seen worship in heaven in a previous vision, but when he saw this worship his breath was taken away by the realization of what he was seeing. He saw the Lamb of God surrounded by the worshippers in heaven.

We began the Book of Revelation with the message to the churches to keep their eyes on Jesus. We see in this vision that the worship in heaven is drawn out of the worshippers because their eyes are on Jesus. There will be the realization that not one of those whom Jesus died to save will have been lost; even those who have come through the worst of the tribulations brought about by Satan and his representatives will be saved. They have been washed in the blood of the Lamb, as John wrote in the first chapter of the Book of Revelation; therefore they are perfectly pure in the eyes of God. There is now no trace of sin in them. They and all they offer to the Lord are perfect before him.

In Chapter 15 of the Book of Revelation John relates that in the worship they are singing a song of Moses and the Lamb. Yet again we cannot escape the clear reference to the Old and New Testament people of God. The people of God before the coming of Jesus and after his coming and return to heaven are one. This vision testifies to the mercy and grace of God expressed in Jesus, the Messiah, who made himself an offering for our sin. He purchased us back from the power of Satan and sin, making reconciliation with God possible again. Paul teaches us in the letter to the Romans that the sacrifice on the Cross was retrospective as well as for all believers in Jesus that are still to come: 'God sacrificed Jesus on the altar of the world to clear that world of sin. Having faith in him sets us in the clear. God decided on this course of action in full view of the public – to set the world in the clear with himself through the sacrifice of Jesus, finally taking care of the sins he had so patiently endured. This is not only clear, but it's now – this is current history! God sets things right. He also makes it possible for us to live in his rightness.'

John is also shown that, right up to the end, the human race will be given the opportunity to respond to this message of salvation if they turn to the Lord in repentance and faith. He is shown three angels going throughout the earth with the message of God for all mankind – the good news of eternal salvation through repentance and faith in Jesus, the warning of the terrible things that must happen on the earth as a result of the sin of the human race, and the pronouncement that there will be a final judgement resulting in an eternal damnation from God for all who have refused to repent and call on the name of the Lord Jesus for salvation. This message, we are told, is the eternal message of God. There is only one message by which we can be saved, and it is the eternal message of God. It is the message the apostles of Jesus were to take to the uttermost parts of the earth. Paul again teaches us of this message in the beginning of the Book of Romans. Paul tells us the message he has been authorized to preach is about what God has done. He wrote that he had been 'authorized as an apostle to proclaim God's words and acts'. He teaches us that this message is about Jesus, the Son of God, as foretold by God in the Old Testament. 'The sacred writings contain preliminary reports by the prophets on God's Son. His descent from David roots him in history; his unique identity as Son of God was shown by the Spirit when Jesus was raised from the dead, setting him apart as the Messiah, our Master.' God guarantees the salvation of all who believingly respond to the message. 'And that's why I can't wait to get to you in Rome, preaching this wonderful good news of God. It's news I'm most proud to proclaim, this extraordinary Message of God's powerful plan to rescue everyone who trusts him, starting with Jews and then right on to everyone else!'

For the encouragement of the churches, John was shown that in all this awesome judgement that will take place the people of God still on earth at the time will 'stand passionately patient, keeping God's commands, staying faithful to Jesus'.

All worship to God is offered by the people of God through Jesus, the Lamb of God – both those in heaven, and in the faithfulness of God's people on earth. There is no other name given under heaven by which we may be saved than that of Jesus.

John is then shown that a time will come when heaven will close its doors to those who have chosen to live their lives for themselves in complete disregard for God and the sacrifice made by the Lord Jesus. The awesome judgements will come upon the earth and no one will be able to prevent them. They will be executed in full – all the righteous judgements of God.

Once again in these visions we are reminded that time and

eternity is a mystery to us. A thousand years is as a day to the Lord, and a day is as a thousand years. There is no past and future; all is now to the Lord. What John was shown is that in all these awesome things that must take place the coming-again of Jesus will take place, and he will be responsible for the separation of the final harvest of the earth.

It is possible, as we have noted before, to try to put these things that must happen into a system of end-time events; but, as I have said previously, I am not qualified for that task. I would ask you to just allow me to put to you that these visions show us that worship of Jesus and faithfulness to him will keep us secure whatever stage we may be at in these things that must take place.

John is told to write to these churches, who are facing persecution from the governing powers, 'I heard a voice out of Heaven, "Write this: Blessed are those who die in the Master from now on; how blessed to die that way!" "Yes," says the Spirit, "and blessed rest from their hard, hard work. None of what they've done is wasted; God blesses them for it all in the end." ' They will be part of the worshipping people of God for eternity, and they know here and now, as they are told of the awesome judgements that are about to take place, that the Judge of all the Earth will do right.

Chapter 11

JUDGEMENT
Revelation 16 and 17

Having been shown the worshipping people of God in heaven and the faithful people of God on earth John was then shown the terrible final judgements of God upon the human race for all their sinful rebellion against him. People of all nations will reap what they have sown. We will also see that judgement takes place both in this life and after death. It all begins with a command from the Throne in heaven: 'I heard a shout of command from the Temple to the Seven Angels: "Begin! Pour out the seven bowls of God's wrath on earth!" ' The churches are encouraged to know that, whatever is happening in the nations of the world, behind them all is the Lord who loved us so much he sent the Son of God to become Jesus, the Lamb of God who takes away the sin of the world. This God is ruling, and nothing happens apart from his allowing or commanding it. As a great powerful king once said, "God raises up whom he will and puts down whom he will." We will be shown here the spiritual forces at work behind the rulers of the world governments, but ultimately God is in control – not man or Satan.

John was told to record the declaration of the angel who is executing these terrible judgements: 'Righteous you are, and your judgements are righteous.' The Judge of all the Earth will do right and at exactly the right time. We are given insight into the Lord taking every detail into account before judgement falls on a people in the account of the fall of Sodom and Gomorrah. The Bible teaches us that he delays judgement, giving people time to repent, but eventually righteous judgement must take place.

In this vision that John recorded for us, the people of the nations of the world begin to experience skin diseases that are repulsive and painful. The nations have caused much pain and revulsion with their sinful actions, and now they are reaping what they have sown. God was grieved by the sinfulness of men's hearts and actions before the Flood. He described the sins of Israel in Isaiah as being like putrefying sores from head to foot. Sin not only pollutes and causes pain to man; it is repulsive and painful to the heart of God. Not only are people directly affected in their health, but the environment is affected as well. The sea is so polluted it begins to thicken up like coagulated blood and the life in the sea begins to die. There is a suddenness about this, and people who have received luxuries of trade by the sea and much good food begin to suffer because of this loss. Not only luxuries are affected; basic drinking water becomes contaminated or is in short supply. Things are so bad that Heaven feels it has to respond. John heard Heaven say it is righteous judgement on the human race, which has so polluted what God made so good in the beginning. The sun becomes so fiercely hot that people are burnt by it. The environment begins to fall apart. The people know it is judgement from God because of their conduct, yet they refuse to repent of their actions. Instead they curse God because of his righteous judgement. Here again the Bible teaches us that the atheist will not succeed in convincing the people of the world there is no God. Even in this suffering they are aware of God and Jesus, the Messiah, the Lamb of God.

Eventually the global systems will begin to collapse and the world powers will turn on one another. The world authorities will fall apart as the environment is also falling apart, yet people will still refuse to accept the Lordship of Jesus and worship God. In fact, even though the global powers begin to fail they will manage to form a war coalition to fight against the people of God, who will come together to survive the persecution of the world systems. We are told a large war party from the east will be able to advance because the Euphrates will have dried up. They will be able to get people of all nations to join in this great war because of evil spiritual influence. Satan will be at work, marshalling his evil powers to make a powerful push against the Lord's people, who will remain a witness for the Lord on earth.

To his people the Lord had John write a warning: 'Keep watch! I come unannounced, like a thief. You're blessed if, awake and dressed, you're ready for me.' The churches then and now need to keep watching and listening to the Holy Spirit. The Lord Jesus himself taught the disciples this while he was here on earth, and he tells John to write in his letters to the churches, 'If you pull the covers back over your head and sleep on, oblivious to God, I'll return when you least expect it, break into your life like a thief in the night.' There will be a great earthquake like the world has never experienced before and will never again experience. The city that is the centre of the global powers will split in three and all the world will feel the effect of this earthquake; yet the Lord had John record that they still will not repent. Even as they experience these terrible catastrophes, the people of the world curse God rather than repent of their sin. John was then told that he would be shown more of the final judgement of God coming upon this great city. The symbols shown to John suggest that two world powers will join together in an effort to silence the testimony of God's people. They will put many of the Lord's people to death. The people who will not accept Jesus as Lord will be dazzled by the power of this system. It will perform great wonders and they will submit to its authority.

Again the Lord warned his churches, "But don't drop your guard. Use your head." The Lord's people of all ages should give careful thought to these things, because we do not know the day or the hour when the Lord will come again. Allow me to remind you of some of the words of the Lord Jesus: "Stay alert; be in prayer so you don't wander into temptation without even knowing you're in danger. There is a part of you that is eager, ready for anything in God. But there's another part that's as lazy as an old dog sleeping by the fire." The apostle Peter wrote, 'Everything in the world is about to be wrapped up, so take nothing for granted. Stay wide-awake in prayer.' The one thing to watch out for is the name of Jesus. Satan hates it. He will allow all kinds of religious parties and festivals, but he will never allow Jesus to be honoured as the true Messiah, the King of Kings and Lord of Lords.

Eventually there will be a falling-out among the world powers. Their systems will divide and they will begin to destroy one another. The environment is breaking up and chaos is being experienced all over the world. The Lord told John to record that still the people of the world would not repent and turn to God for mercy and forgiveness. They will, however, know that it is God they are dealing with – and his Messiah, the Lamb of God, Jesus.

The Lord has given his word that he will watch over his people during these times when terrible things take place. While the judgements of the plagues were taking place in Egypt the Lord watched over his chosen people, and he will do so when the judgements come upon the whole earth. We cannot often understand what is happening, but we do know that we can trust the Lord, who is in control of all things.

We know only too well that it is entirely because of the grace of God that we are saved from being just like them. As Paul teaches us in his letter to the Ephesians, 'It wasn't so long ago that you were mired in that old stagnant life of sin. You let the world, which doesn't know the first thing about living, tell you how to live. You filled your lungs with polluted unbelief, and then exhaled disobedience. We all did it, all of us doing what we felt like doing, when we felt like doing it, all of us in the same boat. It's a wonder God didn't lose his temper and do away with the whole lot of us.'

Just and righteous laws have never proved able to change those who choose to ignore them when their own personal gain is at risk. The human race is so given over to sin that it hates God and his righteousness and will do all it can to fight against him.

John was also shown that the rule of the governments of the world 'fell into sudden eclipse'. All rule will be thrown out; the human race will not fear God or the rule of human law. They will become greedy, merciless, and cruel as wolves, tearing into the poor and feasting on them. 'Shredding the needy to pieces only to discard them' is the way one of the scriptures describes them. They are without the restraint of any law.

In Chapter 16, Verse 12 the Middle East is again brought to our attention: 'the great Euphrates River: It dried up to nothing. The dry riverbed became a fine roadbed for the kings from the East.' Fifty years ago, while I was under conviction of sin and beginning to seek God, an elder in a local church invited me to go to his home on Friday evenings to study the Bible. Often he would say to me, "Look at this map on the front page of our daily newspapers; look at the maps in the back of your Bible. They are the same maps." He would go on to say that he believed the Bible teaches us that the Middle East will become more and more the focus of the attention of the world powers and the scene of the final struggles of the end times. I have noticed that in the last fifty years the Middle East has hardly been out of the news. Abraham's bloodline, through Isaac and Jacob and through Ishmael and Esau have had to be included in the thinking of the world powers. I wonder if the mention of the kings from the East brought to your mind, as to mine, the fact that the East is increasingly said to be the emerging world power. We may not be able to say what stage we are at in the things that must take place before Jesus comes again, but it is amazing how prominent the change of world power is. Environmental concern increases along with the uncertainty of the global financial crisis. It would be strange indeed if anyone reading seriously through the Book of Revelation could miss the fact that there is to be an earthquake that will affect the whole earth. It will cause the hearts of the human race to fail with fear, and yet people continue to curse God. I can recall, as many of you will, the tsunami that actually very slightly moved the earth on its axis and all the lives that were lost. It was during the Christmas season, but, in spite of the news coverage of the terrible devastation, it was soon forgotten and life went on as before.

So in this vision John was shown again the battle taking place between God and Satan, and the choice people have to follow one or the other. It may seem at times as if Satan with all the kingdoms of this world dancing to his tune is going to win, but the Lord revealed to John that it would be the Lamb of God, the Lord Jesus Christ, who would ultimately win and provide for his people for eternity.

John was then shown in more detail these final events.

Chapter 12

DOOM
Revelation 18 and 19

John had been shown the terrible judgements that are to come upon the human race and then, in Chapter 18 of the Book of Revelation, he was shown in another vision the doom of the centre of the global powers. It is not a message that the world wants to hear; it is hope of things getting better that the people of this world want to hear. We do not have enough information to be able to say when this will happen, but we are told it surely will happen. The nations, coming together, may think they have found a global system that will bring peace and prosperity, but the message of the Lord is that this system is doomed. If all the hope we have is in this world, then we are bound to dismiss this message. The people in Noah's day rejected the preaching of Noah, but the doom eventually came – and just when they were least expecting it. The people of God are told to keep their eyes open and to watch for the signs of the coming-again of the Lord Jesus; and among the signs is a coming-together of the nations in a global system that they feel does not need God. The message is so sure that the Lord puts it in the past tense. The word used by the Lord is *ruined*. 'Ruined, ruined, Great Babylon, ruined! A ghost town for demons is all that's left!' How many cities of the rulers of world powers have been a testimony to this? Places once the glory of powerful nations are now deserted. This great city – the centre of the global world system – will not only be devoid of human life; it will be inhabited by evil spirits, making it too dreadful a place to be inhabited.

The Bible, from the Book of Genesis onwards, speaks of Babylon as a symbol of human rebellion against God. In this vision given to John the rebellion has become global and all nations are governed by a central power that demands that it be treated as God, governing what people may do and buy. The human race is mesmerized by this global centre that offers peace and prosperity to all who give allegiance to it. It has the potential to provide all it promises, but it demands body-and-soul commitment to it. All the rulers of the world have given allegiance to this global power; and so have all the commercial traders, because they make great profits by her. Here is the final world trade centre. The human race begins to believe it has found the answer to peace without God. It allows the human race to indulge all the sinful desires of the heart, as they did before the Flood in Noah's time. John was told, of this centre of globalization, 'All nations drank the wild wine of her whoring; kings of the earth went whoring with her; entrepreneurs made millions exploiting her.' And, 'Her sins stink to high Heaven; God has remembered every evil she's done.' This is the view God has of this global system. The world will glory in it because it allows all that selfish sinful nature desires. Paul, writing of the human race, said that they glory in their shame and boast of the wickedness they have practised and think they have got away with. God is grieved by the evil which man is glorying in and which he invents new ways to practise.

The amazing thing John was shown next is that some of the Lord's people become so engrossed in the system that the Lord has to send messengers to warn them to get out of it while they still can: 'Get out, my people, as fast as you can, so you don't get mixed up in her sins, so you don't get caught in her doom.' What a warning this is to the local churches!

They have already been told to wake up and be attentive to what the Spirit is saying. Allow me to ask you, dear reader, have you ever thought it is possible to become desensitized to the Holy Spirit? Samson, we are told, got up to go and did not realize the Lord was not with him as before. There is a danger of losing that first-love relationship with the Lord Jesus. Do not think, the apostle Peter wrote, that because the Lord delays giving time to repent he will not in the end act in righteous judgement.

The judgement will come and it will be swift and complete. The world rulers will mourn because of the total ruin of this great world trade centre. John was shown them crying out: 'Everything you've lived for, gone! . . . Doom, doom, the great city doomed! Dressed in the latest fashions, adorned with the finest jewels, in one hour such wealth wiped out!' This doom of a globalized system governing the nations is among the things that must take place before Jesus comes again. It will be swift (like lightning) and unexpected (like a thief), but it will surely come.

The local churches have to live in this world, but they must not follow the principles of the selfish, greedy ways of the world. They have heard the word of the Lord: "What good would it do to get everything you want and lose you, the real you?" What a price for the temporary things of this life!

In this vision, while those who chose to follow the ways of this global system mourn their terrible loss, the Lord tells his people to rejoice because justice is finally done; those who have bought and sold the souls of the human race have finally reaped what they have sown. This great global system will not only trade in material things and the bodies of people, but it will also trade in religion, taking over the bodies and souls of people. It will be so powerful and deceptive that the Lord's people will need powerful preachers to warn them of the error of dealing with this system. They will remind the churches of the words of Jesus: "You can't worship two gods at once.

Loving one god, you'll end up hating the other. Adoration of one feeds contempt for the other. You can't worship God and Money." The challenge of Joshua will also be brought to them: "If you decide that it's a bad thing to worship GOD, and then choose a god you'd rather serve – and do it today. . . . As for me and my family, we'll worship GOD." There came a time when the Jewish believers had to choose between staying in Jerusalem or leaving, as the Lord Jesus had said they would have to if they were to avoid the judgement coming on the city. When the captain gives the command to abandon ship it is time to leave.

Those who passionately love the Lord Jesus, and follow him in obedience that comes from faith and works by love, will, unlike the other people of the world, rejoice over the fall of this wicked, godless system.

Come with me now into Chapter 19 of the Book of Revelation. Here John describes a vision in which he sees rejoicing, and the cause of the rejoicing is the salvation of God. God's people know that salvation comes from God himself through the Lord Jesus Christ. John was made aware of this in Chapter 5 of the Book of Revelation, where the occupants of heaven worship the Lord for his salvation through the Cross of the Lord Jesus. 'The slain Lamb is worthy!' Jesus taught the disciples while he was here on earth to rejoice that their names were written in heaven. In this vision, John sees they are worshipping the Lord for his justice on all who have chosen to follow their own sinful, selfish nature rather than accept Jesus as Lord and Saviour. They are singing, "Hallelujah! The salvation and glory and power are God's – his judgements true, his judgements just." It is the justice of God they celebrate, not the awful destiny of those who have rejected the loving salvation God offered them.

John is shown that all these things are linked to the coming-again of the Lord Jesus. The order of the events may be debated, but the fact is that Jesus is coming again. When he does, his people will rejoice in him and his great salvation and justice. They will celebrate with him the eternal union between Jesus and his people. It is this that will be celebrated by the people of God, not the terrible destiny that the human race has brought upon itself. The Bible teaches us that they will reap what they sow. The blood of Abel cried out for this justice along with all the blood of the martyrs. I do not know how – and I cannot point to a scripture that teaches it – but I think God will in some way wipe from the minds of his people the awful destiny of those who have rejected God.

In the next vision, the Lord showed John that the human race will be given one last chance to experience eternity with him. They will, at the close of this time, be given an opportunity to choose between God's way and Satan's way.

Chapter 13

CHOOSE WHOM YOU WILL SERVE
Revelation 20

In Chapter 20 of the Book of Revelation we have a vision that has caused a lot of debate over the years. I am not able to offer any thoughts that have not already been offered; they are available in many books. I would like to ask you to consider that Revelation 20 clearly has three parts to it: the 1,000 years of Satan being bound, his release after the 1,000 years, and the final judgement at the great white Throne.

John had been shown the global rule of the world system and its rebellion against God. The people in all the nations of the world have had the gospel preached to them, but many of them have chosen the rule of Satan rather than the Lordship of Jesus. In Revelation 20 the one behind the world system, Satan, is put out of action for 1,000 years. In his place the Lord himself sets up a righteous global rule. The rule of God is applied with zero tolerance to the whole of the human race. It is the rule of righteousness, not the rule of human rights. God will decide what can and cannot be done, what can and cannot be watched. After the 1,000 years, Satan is released and allowed to present his case again for rebellion against God. The human race is given the choice: God and his Messiah, Jesus, or Satan. The human race chooses Satan and sets out to remove all trace of God and his people from the earth, but God at this point says, "Enough!" and he steps in with a final judgement on Satan that is irreversible.

In the light of this vision, may I ask you to consider again the vital importance of giving careful thought to the message that God has for the whole of the human race. I can only write for those who believe there is a God; I am not capable of convincing those who do not believe God exists. In fact, the Bible tells us, 'Anyone who wants to approach God must believe both that he exists and that he cares enough to respond to those who seek him.' So I urge those who believe God exists to consider the message of salvation that is given to us in the Bible. We do not have to feel we are sinners; God tells us we are. It is not a matter of what we feel or think; the issue is what God says. Eternity depends on believing God and responding to him, or rejecting him and what he says. One thing is absolutely clear in this last book of the Bible: judgement and Judgement Day are coming, and everyone will give an account of themselves to God.

As we read John's account of this vision we are looking for the message that the Lord Jesus has for the local churches that will be a lamp to their feet and a light to their path as they live for him.

The message in this vision is that there is a specific period of time that has a beginning and ending and it is under the control of the Lord. We are told six times it will be 1,000 years. It will begin with an angel coming down from heaven. He will have been given a task from the Throne in heaven.

The Devil is to be chained and placed in a deep pit from which he cannot have any influence over people of the world. The chain in the angel's hand may well be symbolic of the Holy Spirit. On one occasion, when Paul was being held prisoner by the Romans because of the accusations of the Jews, he said, "I go bound in the Spirit to Rome." There may be human hands or circumstances involved, but they are being used by the Holy Spirit. Jesus himself demonstrated that under the Holy Spirit he went out into the desert and at the right time sent the Devil packing. In the words of one of his parables, 'He bound the strong man and then began to release those that had been bound by him.'

This vision shows that the people on earth at this time will be given the opportunity to live under the Lordship of Jesus without any influence from Satan. They will experience what it is like to have to conform to his will, living as he would have them live – not by human ideas of what is right, but by righteousness. Whatever their response to this may be, it will not be because of the Devil. This is made clear to John in the vision by the setting up of thrones on the earth from which righteous judgement will be exercised over the nations of the world. There will be a global government by God. The nations have had in the past a global government by the Devil and those who follow him. Now they have the opportunity to experience the contrast between the government of God and the government of the Devil. As he looked at this vision, John was made aware that some of the people he saw were those who had been put to death because of their faith in Jesus. They had been made alive again, just as the Lord Jesus raised Lazarus from the dead; but these, John is told, will never die again. They had eternal life given to them when they believed that Jesus is the Christ the Son of God and their saviour. They held to the Lordship of Jesus and would not conform to the ways of the world, even though it cost them their lives. History tells us that from the time that John wrote down this vision, and up to the present day, people who have come to faith in Jesus have been put to death because of their faith. They will be among the ones reigning with Jesus on the earth for a specific period of time.

The Lord Jesus, through his angel, also makes clear in this vision that the remainder of the dead will not be raised to life at this time. John is then told to write, 'This is the first resurrection . . .' So much has been written about what this means, and there have been many debates about how many resurrections there will be. Well, there will be at least two. The message to the churches suffering persecution is that those who have been put to death for their faith have not missed out in any way. I believe Abel will be among those who are there reigning with Jesus in that period of time, for he was accepted because of his faith in the sacrifice he brought to God for his sins. What he brought represented in shadow form the sacrifice to be made by the Lord Jesus on the Cross. The Bible teaches us, I believe, that all who are the children of God are his children through faith in the sacrifice he made for us in the Lord Jesus. Whether they looked forward to it or back to it makes no difference; it is because of the precious blood of Jesus that people become the people of God. John was also made aware that all people will one day be raised to life and that they will have to give an account of themselves to God.

John is also shown that his people will reign with him as priests. This is a great comfort to the churches that are now a kingdom of priests but are despised by the world and rejected like their Lord is. They are often ruled by unrighteous government and prevented from functioning as the Lord would have them do. As the wise man wrote in one of his proverbs, 'When the wicked rule the righteous are hidden.' They are often hidden in prisons or prevented from speaking because their words would offend the rulers of the world system.

We may consider here that there are times when the Lord will grant that two or three gathered in his name in prayer may bind on earth and it will be bound in heaven. The apostles taught, 'But you are the ones chosen by God, chosen for the high calling of priestly work, chosen to be a holy people, God's instruments to do his work and speak out for him, to tell others of the night-and-day difference he made for you – from nothing to something, from rejected to accepted.' Examples of this are given in the Book of Acts and church history. Though they are few and infrequent they are a reminder that there is a time coming when it will be the norm for the people of God to rule on the earth over the nations of the world. Now may be the time of Satan and the world systems, but the time is limited and under the control of the Lord.

John was told to record for us that this time will end and Satan will be set free again. He will immediately use his deception on the people of the world to try to convince those who have not accepted the Lordship of Jesus that he has a better way that gives them all they want. The issue is whether Jesus is Lord. Some will want to decide their own rights. They will think that human rights not righteousness is what is best for them. What Satan will offer them is the very same thing he offered to Adam and Eve. This will lead to a worldwide revolt against the Lord. Satan will be behind a final world war that will have as its motive the removal of all influence from God through Jesus and his people. But God himself will intervene before they are able to destroy his people. His rule will be maintained through Jesus and his people. After this awesome time God will judge Satan and his representatives, and he will cast them into hell. He will set up his final judgement (seen in the symbolic form of a great white Throne, representing righteous and pure judgement). We may note that there are not many thrones – just the one sole authority and sovereign ruler: God.

We often speak of the need for a clear paper trail when dealing with issues. Well, God will have an irrefutable paper trail recorded in a book that will demonstrate beyond all dispute that his judgement is absolutely righteous. Every opposition will be silenced; no word will be able to be raised against his judgement; there will be no room for cover-ups. The Judge of all the Earth will be seen to do what is right. Righteousness and purity will triumph in the end, and God's people will be presented faultless before the Throne of his glory with great joy.

Their names will be written in the book of life. They will

have believed the Lord Jesus is the Christ, the Son of God, and through believing they will have found life in him.

The awesome message of this vision is that after every opportunity to repent of sin and receive Jesus as Lord and Saviour people will choose sin and Satan; they will choose the systems of this world government rather than righteousness. The Bible teaches us that now, today, is always the time to be saved – we have no guarantee the offer will be there tomorrow. We have a choice: now to accept the Lordship of Jesus, or please ourselves, our own egos and appetites. In this vision, as throughout the Bible, God reveals to us clearly that our eternal destiny is decided by the choice we make. There are two possible destinies for everyone: to be with the Lord and his people for eternity, or go to hell with Satan and all who choose his alternative of self-satisfying rather than God-pleasing.

The Lord makes it clear in the Bible that what he is looking for is obedience that comes from faith and works by love, a passionate love for Jesus that puts him first in all things.

In the next chapter of the Book of Revelation John tells us of another vision of the eternal destiny of the people of God.

Chapter 14

ETERNITY: ALL THINGS NEW
Revelation 21 and 22

Having travelled through the Book of Revelation this far, we understand that God has both the right and the ability to make all things new again. He created them in the first place, and through the Cross of the Lord Jesus Christ he paid a redemption price and made restoration of all things to their state before the Fall. All things will be again without sin, only now there will never again be the possibility of sin entering because of the atonement made by the Lord Jesus Christ on the Cross.

What a wonderful inheritance the Lord Jesus has prepared for his people – an eternity to look forward to! I recall while doing door-to-door evangelism meeting two men in one morning that brought home to me this wonderful truth. The first man (in his eighties) when I asked about the future said, "For a man in his eighties it does not bear thinking about." A few doors along the road I met another man (also in his eighties) and he said to me, "I am looking forward to being with the Lord for eternity, and I am thankful for the life he has given me so far." What a sad thing for a person to arrive at eighty years of age and have no future to look forward to! What a joy to be able to say, "I know that Jesus, whom I have trusted with my life, has prepared an eternity for me also." He was simply saying what the Bible teaches us: that the work God has begun, and it will be completed when Jesus returns again.

There will be beauty, equality, splendour, love, no consequences of sin, life, freshness, holiness, reconciliation and worship – an eternity of unbroken service in a place of complete satisfaction for God and his people. This city is a place, but it is also a people – the people of God from the Old and New Testaments. The foreshadowing of these things should be seen in the local churches now.

You may like, as you read this chapter, to ask the question (if you have never done so before), whom do I want to be with for eternity? – especially as we consider John's record of the last invitation.

John was then shown another vision. This time it is of a new heaven and a new earth. The previous vision ended with more detail of the destiny of those whose names are not written in the Lamb's book of life. Having been shown that awesome scene, John was now shown the wonderful destiny of the Lord's people. A new heaven and earth created by the Lord is shown to John. In the Message translation, John tells us that the old heaven and earth are gone; there is no trace of them. He then becomes aware that on the new earth there is no sea (so I presume the land mass will be greatly increased). Then John saw the New Jerusalem coming down out of heaven. The city of God and his people are to occupy the new earth. It seems it is not the old Jerusalem and the Jewish people; it is the New Heavenly Jerusalem and the newly created people of God from among the Jews and the Gentiles. The Lord then states to John again that he is the one who is the beginning of all things and he is also the consummation of all things. What John was being shown is the inheritance of the Lord's passionately faithful people. The churches facing struggles within and trials without have all this to look forward to. The Lord then told John that this is not the final destiny of the entire human race. Those who have chosen to live for the lust of the flesh and the pride of life will spend eternity with one another in the lake of fire.

The Lord Jesus said to the disciples in the upper room before he went to the Cross, "There is plenty of room for you in my Father's home. If that weren't so, would I have told you that I'm on my way to get a room ready for you?" In this final vision Jesus showed something of the wonder of that place prepared for his people to spend eternity with him. John tells us, 'I saw Heaven and earth new-created. Gone the first Heaven, gone the first earth . . .'

I ask you to consider that we are not going up to heaven to be with God. God is coming to spend eternity with us on a newly created earth. In the beginning God walked with Adam and Eve, before their fall into sin and the government of Satan. He will walk with all his people again on the redeemed earth. John tells us that the occupants of heaven marvel at this sight: "Look! Look! God has moved into the neighbourhood, making his home with men and women! They're his people, he's their God. He'll wipe every tear from their eyes. Death is gone for good – tears gone, crying gone, pain gone – all the first order of things gone."

This revelation comes to a conclusion with all the consequences of sin removed forever from the experience of God's people. The people of God with their new resurrection bodies, like the Lord Jesus after his resurrection, will be able to live on earth or go to heaven. They will be as God intended them to be – the managers of his creation in an unbroken relationship with him.

Come with me and see what the Lord Jesus then showed John about the new things that will exist in the New Jerusalem, heaven and earth. I wonder if the 'Water-of-Life River, crystal bright' that John saw shows us a new relationship between heaven and earth. The two mingled together, the water flowed from the Throne and 'right down the middle of the street'. The city is the new city, but the Throne will be the same eternal Throne John saw previously in heaven. John saw another new thing: the Tree of Life that had been in the Garden of Eden was also here, but it was no longer just one tree. The Tree of Life was on either side of the river. Many years ago we lived in Rowan Drive, and on either side of the road rowan trees had been planted. In the New Jerusalem, with the River of Life running through it, the Tree of Life is planted on either side of the river, making easy access for everyone. The fruit is always fresh and gives to the people of every nation equal health.

The next new thing that John was shown is that 'Never again will anything be cursed.' Complete restoration will be accomplished by the Lord Jesus and there will be no possibility of sin entering into the new creation. The new creation is not just a restoration to what Adam lost in the fall; it will be impossible for sin to bring about the curse ever again. The experience described by the apostle Paul will never again be the experience of the people of God. He wrote, 'Something has gone wrong deep within me and gets the better of me every time. It happens so regularly that it's predictable. The moment I decide to do well, sin is there to trip me up. I truly delight in God's commands, but it's pretty obvious that not all of me join in that delight. Parts of me covertly rebel, and just when I least expect it, they take charge. I've tried everything and nothing helps. I'm at the end of my rope. Is there no one who can do anything for me?' Yes, the Bible declares, there is. God has done for us what we could not do for ourselves. He loved the world so much he gave the Son of God, the Lord Jesus Christ, to die for our sins. That atoning sacrifice was a once-for-all-time sacrifice, cleansing away all the consequences of sin forever. The believer in Jesus can say there is even now no condemnation for those who are in Christ Jesus. John was able to see that the people of God see God face-to-face and are able to offer him perfect worship through unbroken communion. They will be in the image of God, mirroring his nature. They will also rule with the Lord, as he intended Adam to, in everlasting light – because the other new thing is that there will be no darkness at all.

John was told at this point that the visions were completed and that they are absolutely reliable, just as the other prophecies in the scripture have proved to be true. We can read of Jeremiah prophesying that the Jews will be taken into captivity by the Babylonians for seventy years and then return to the land, and they did just that. So too these things will happen just as God said. "Tell them", Jesus says through the angel, "that I am on my way. Keep looking for me and doing whatever I tell you." The Message translates the words as ' "Yes, I'm on my way!" Blessed be the one who keeps the words of the prophecy of this book.' John responded just as we should, with worship for all that he has seen and heard. We must make sure not to make the same mistake John did and worship the messenger rather than the one who is the source of the message. We can understand John's response, having been in the presence of this angel who had shown him so much and told him so much, but the angel would not allow it for a moment. The apostle Paul had to warn the church in Corinth that they were putting some of the messengers of the Lord in the place of the Lord himself and it was resulting in division in the church. Paul appeals to them to keep their eyes on Jesus and the Cross. John is told to repeat the warnings that are in this book to those who reject God and choose to glory in sin, so that their eyes will turn to Jesus again. "I, Jesus, sent my Angel to testify to these things for the churches. I'm the Root and Branch of David, the Bright Morning Star." The Lord Jesus himself signs off the wonderful Book of Revelation, stating that he is the Messiah and the herald of the new day that one day will dawn, when all that is recorded in this book has taken place.

Then, having completed the revelation, the final appeal to the human race is given by the Lord: ' "Come!" say the Spirit and the Bride. Whoever hears, echo, "Come!" is anyone thirsty? Come! All who will, come and drink, Drink freely of the Water of Life!'

Before John wrote his final words the Lord instructed him to write, 'I give fair warning to all who hear the words of the prophecy of this book: If you add to the words of this prophecy, God will add to your life the disasters written in this book; if you subtract from the words of the book of this prophecy, God will subtract your part from the Tree of Life and the Holy City that are written in this book.'

Now the final promise of the Bible: 'He who testifies to all these things says it again: "I'm on my way! I'll be there soon!" ' Keep living each day in the light of the coming-again of Jesus. John records for us his personal response: 'Yes! Come, Master Jesus.' The revelation and the Bible are then brought to a close with the words, 'The grace of the Master Jesus be with all of you. Oh, Yes!'

Jesus is coming again, John declared at the beginning of the Book of Revelation. He was shown and recorded for us the things that must happen before Jesus comes again. Some we can clearly see have been happening from the time of the fall of the Roman Empire; others we may be seeing the beginnings of in the nations of the world. What a wonderful joy to be able to say that when Jesus comes again, and time will be no more, "I will be there on the new earth to see the Lord face-to-face and live with him for eternity," because the grace of the Lord Jesus Christ has been with us and will be with us forever.